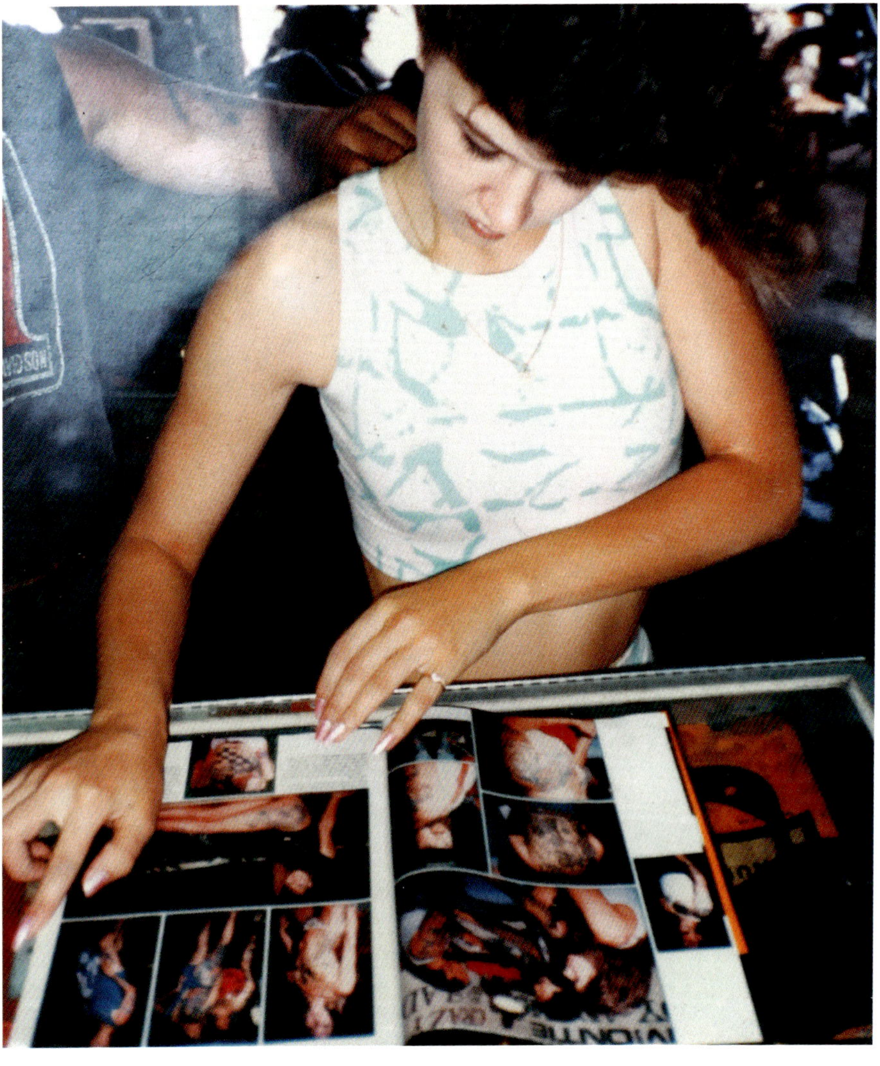

Lisa Kereszi

The more I learn about Women,

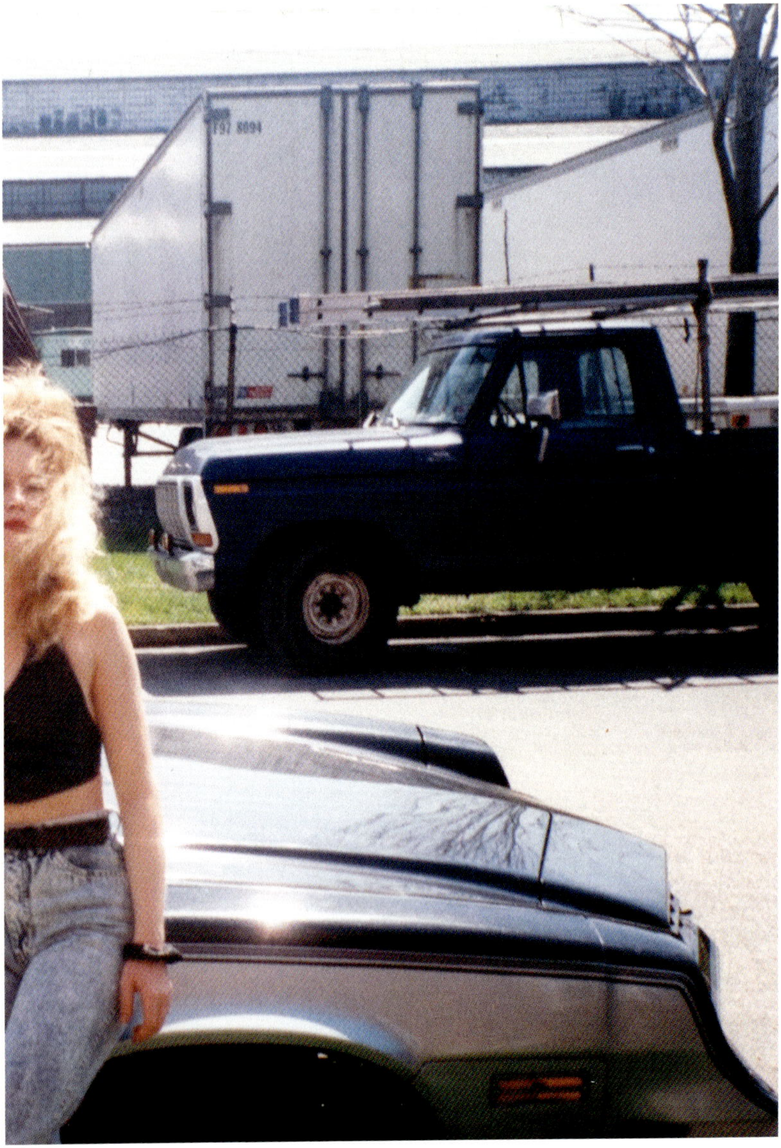

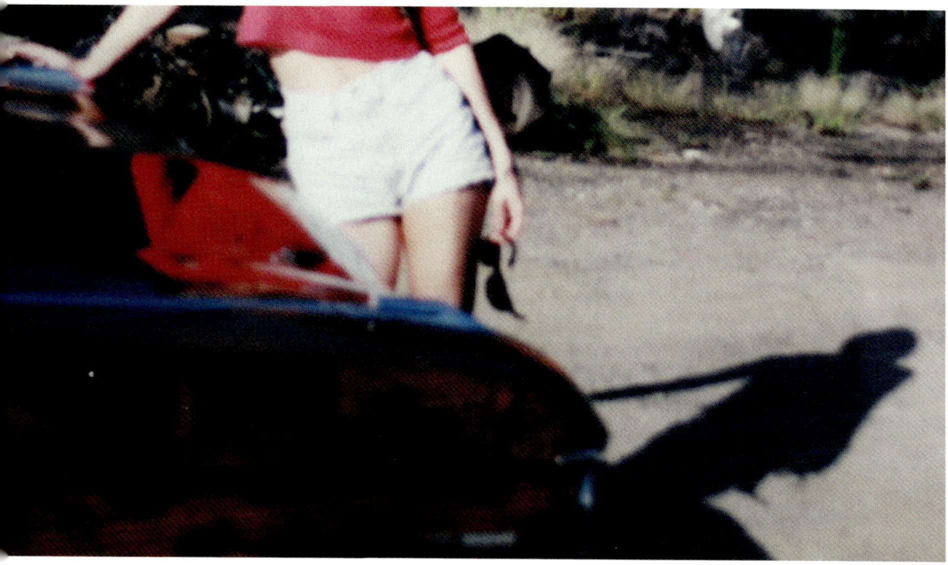

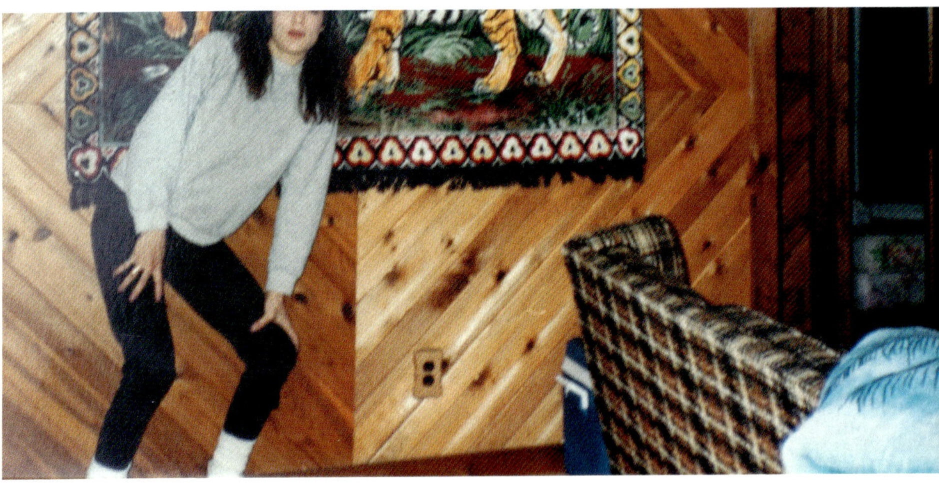

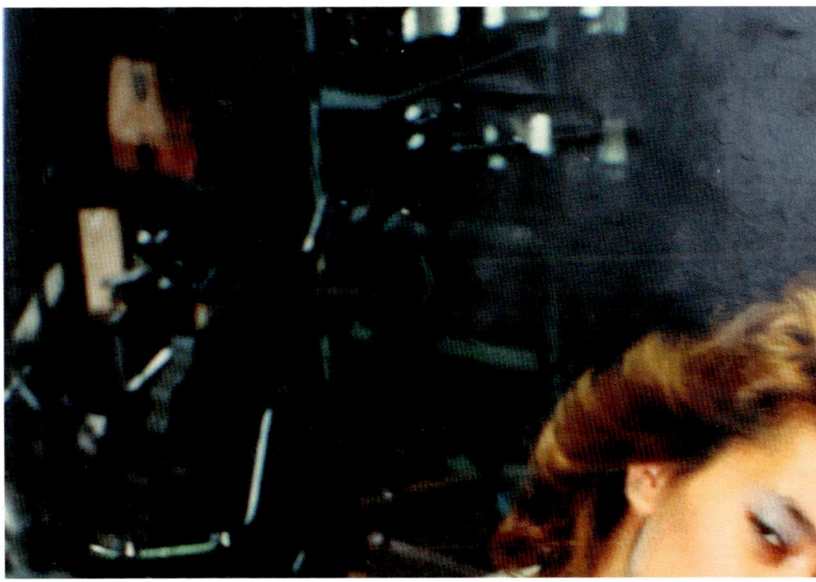

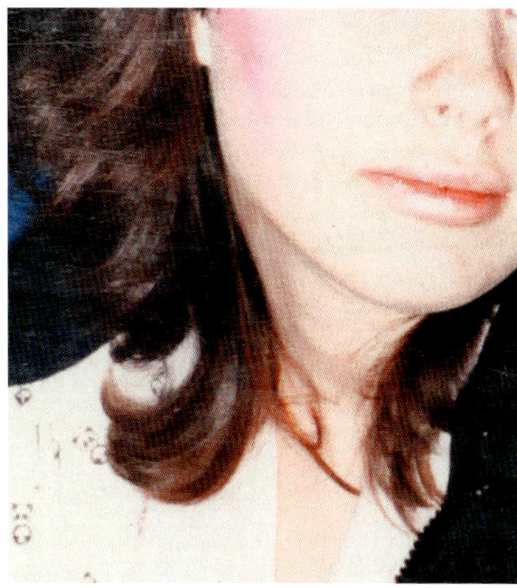

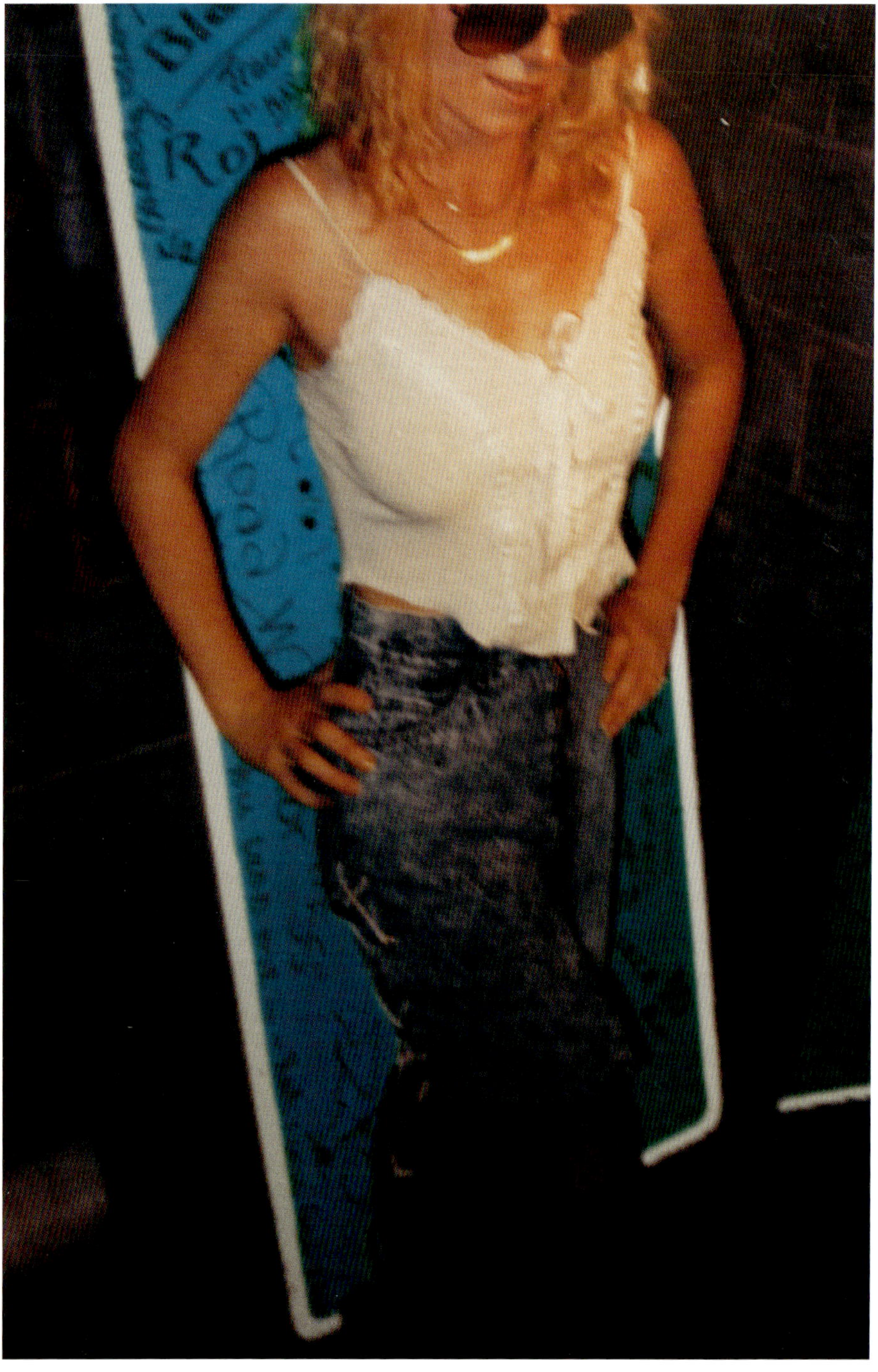

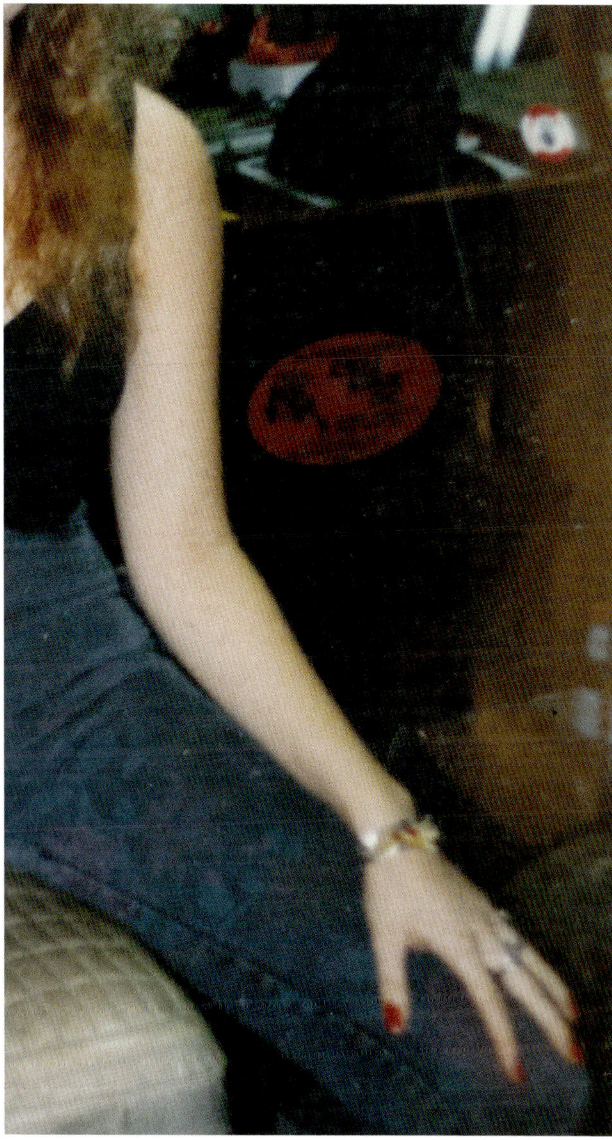

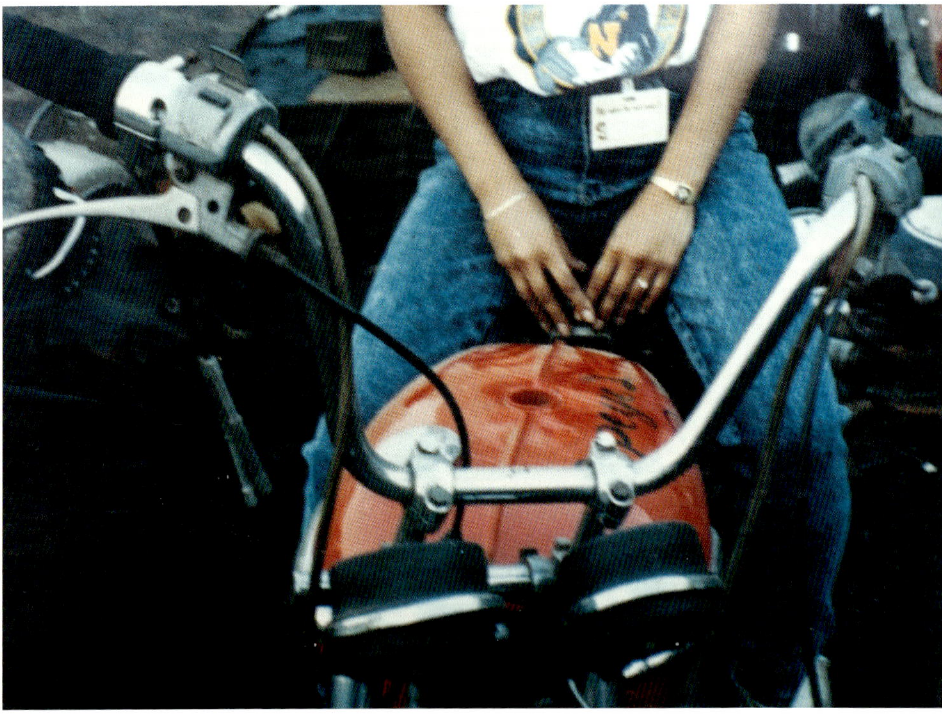

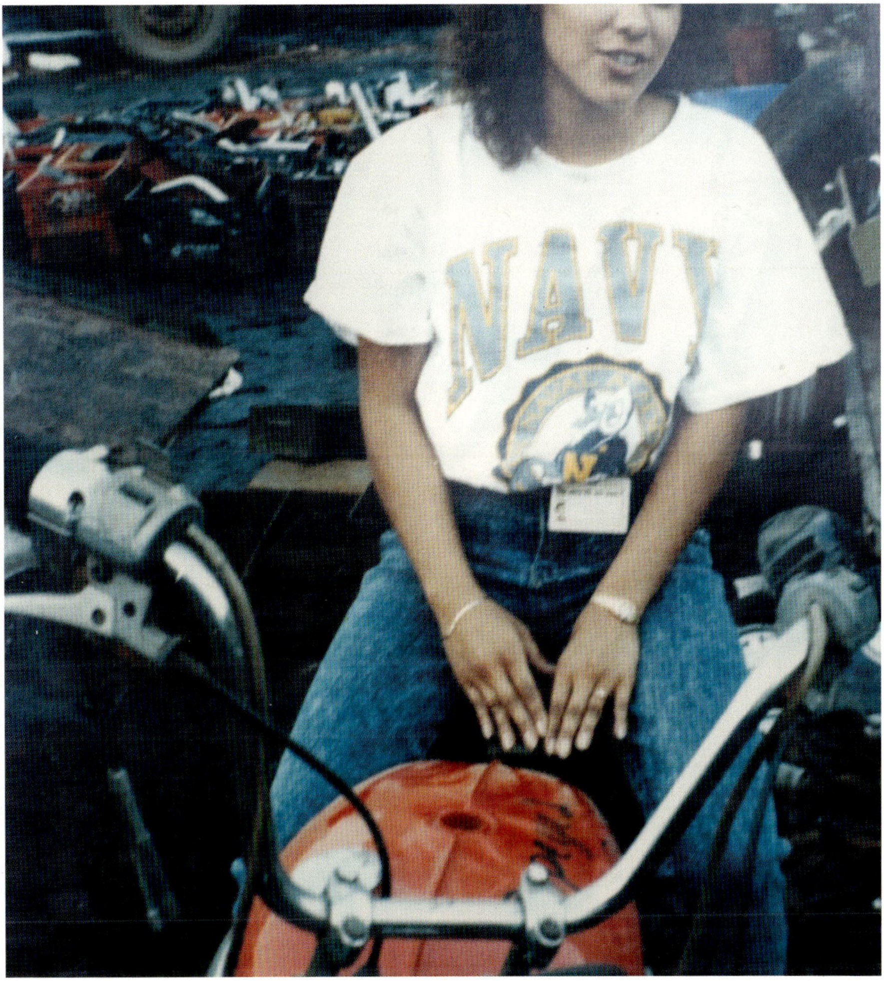
NAV

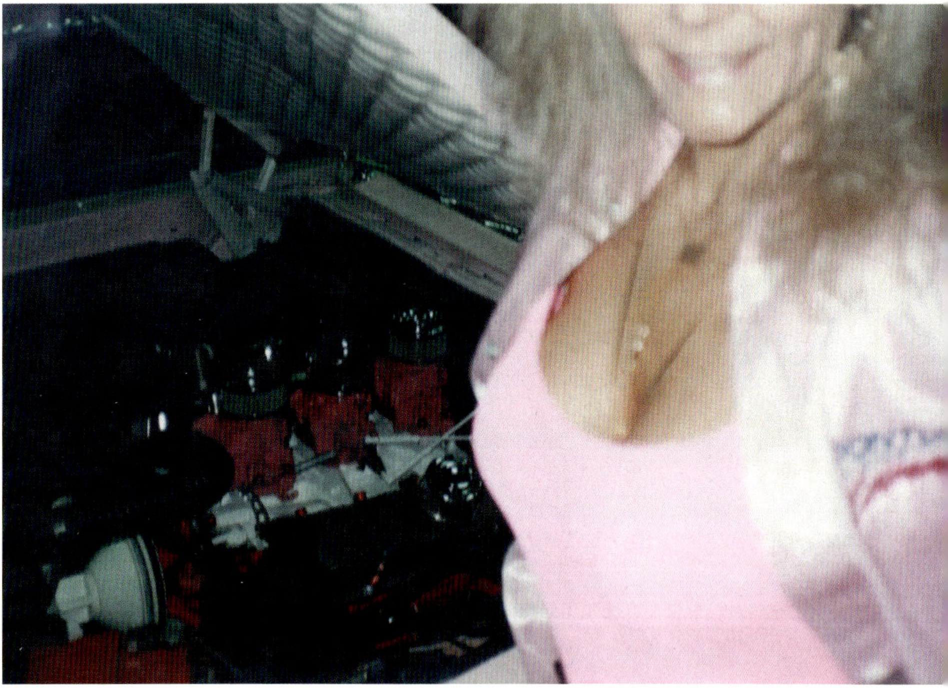

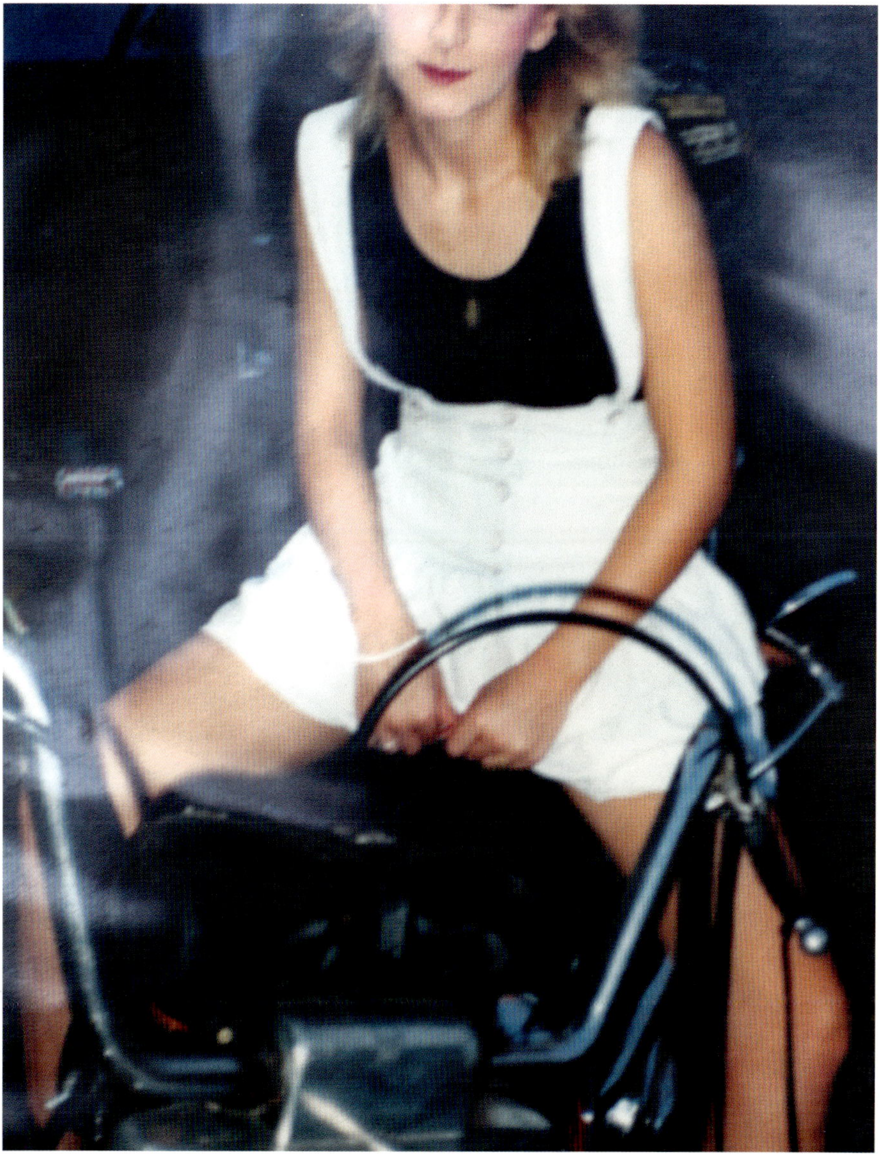

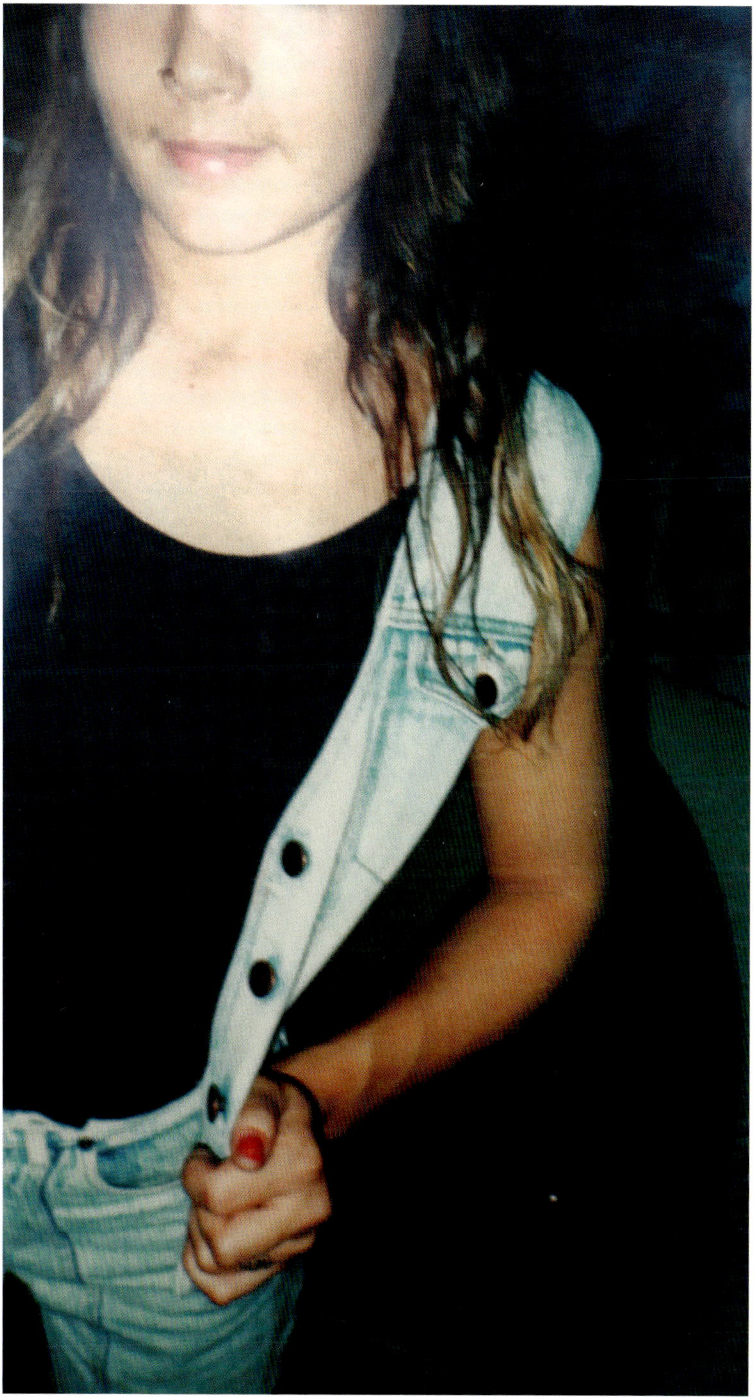

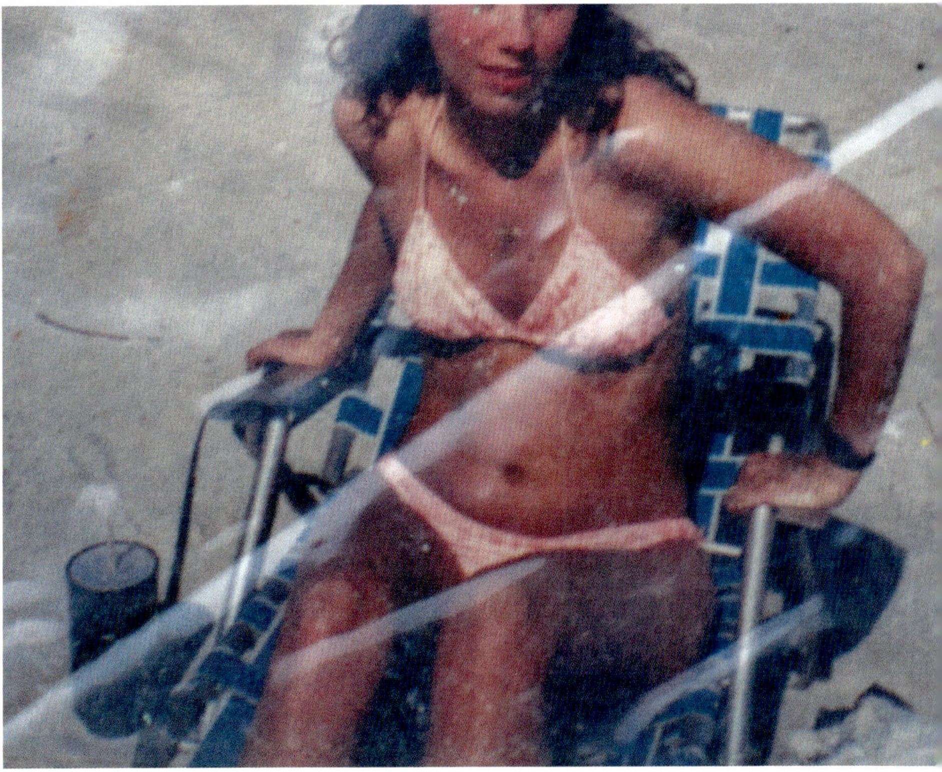

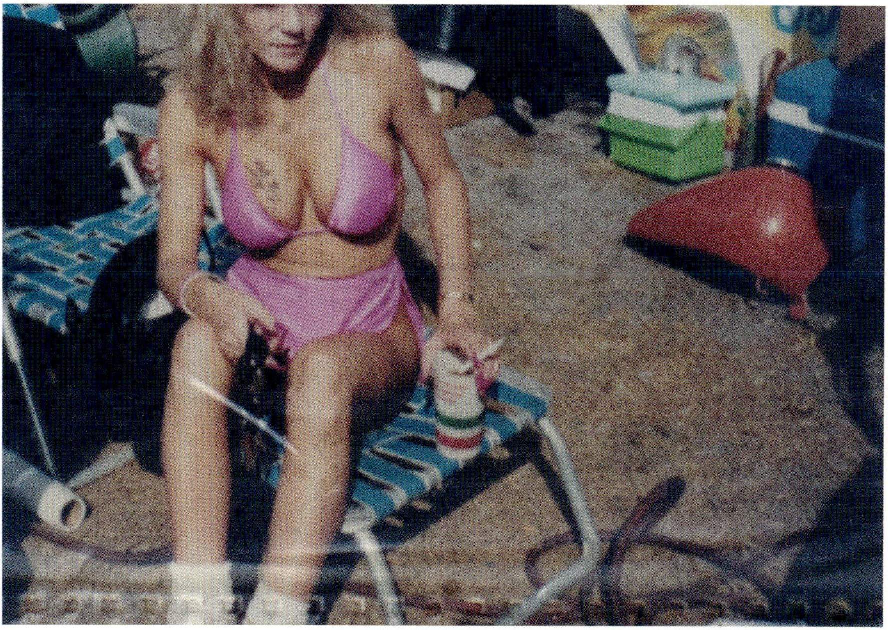

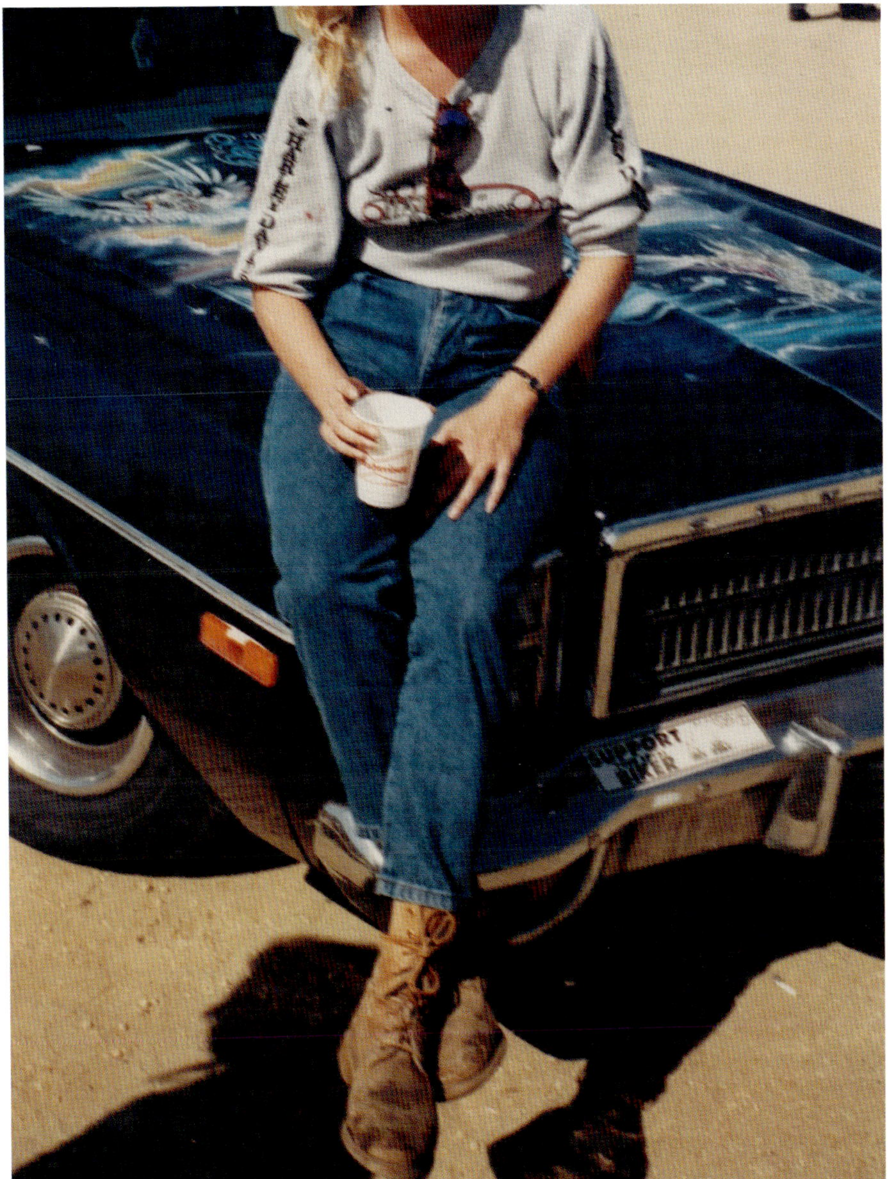
SUPPORT
BIKER

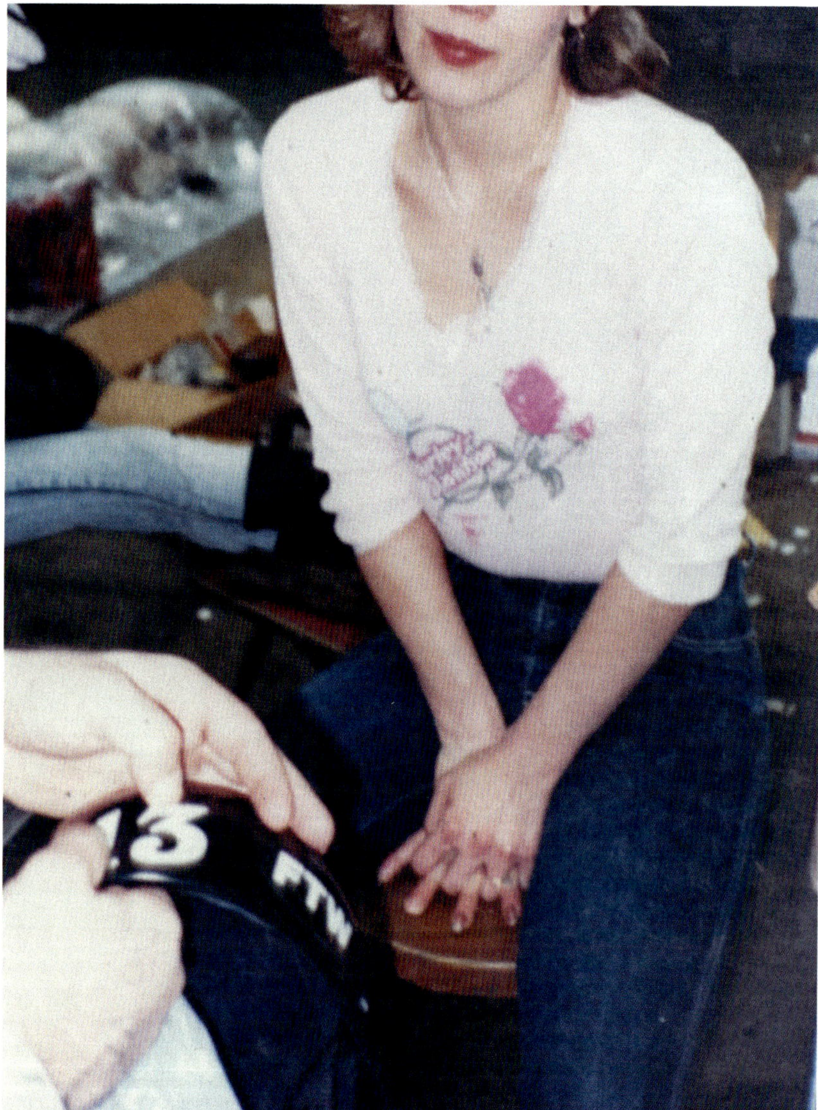
13
FTW

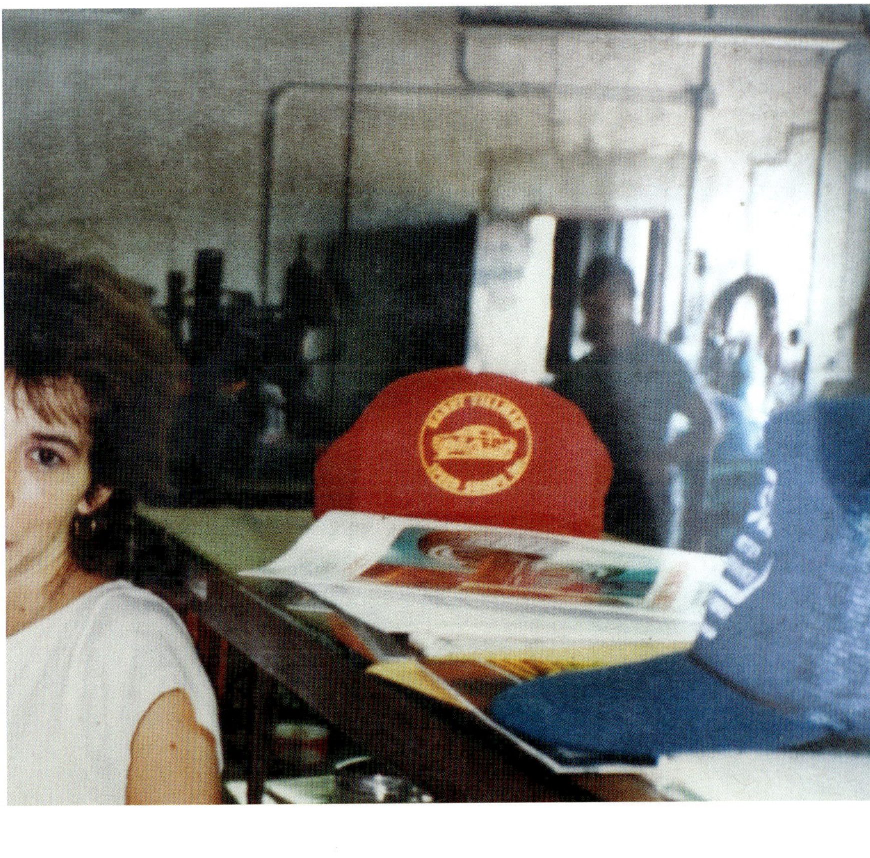

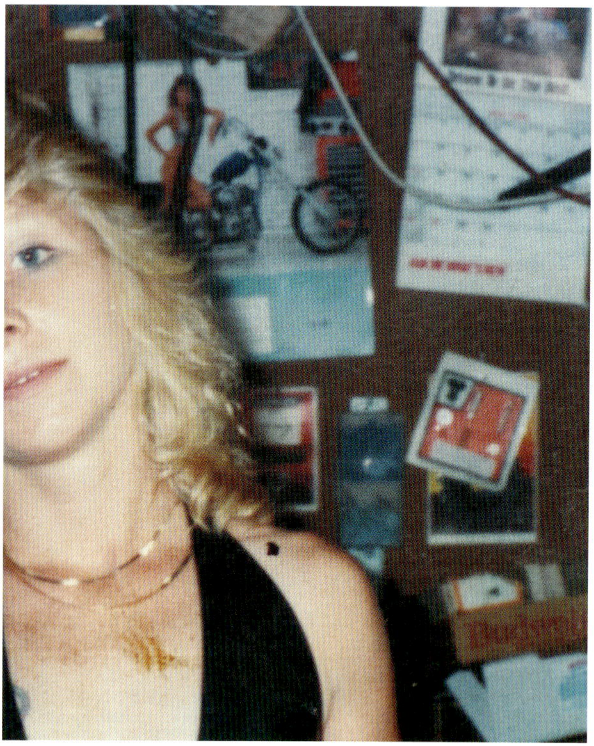

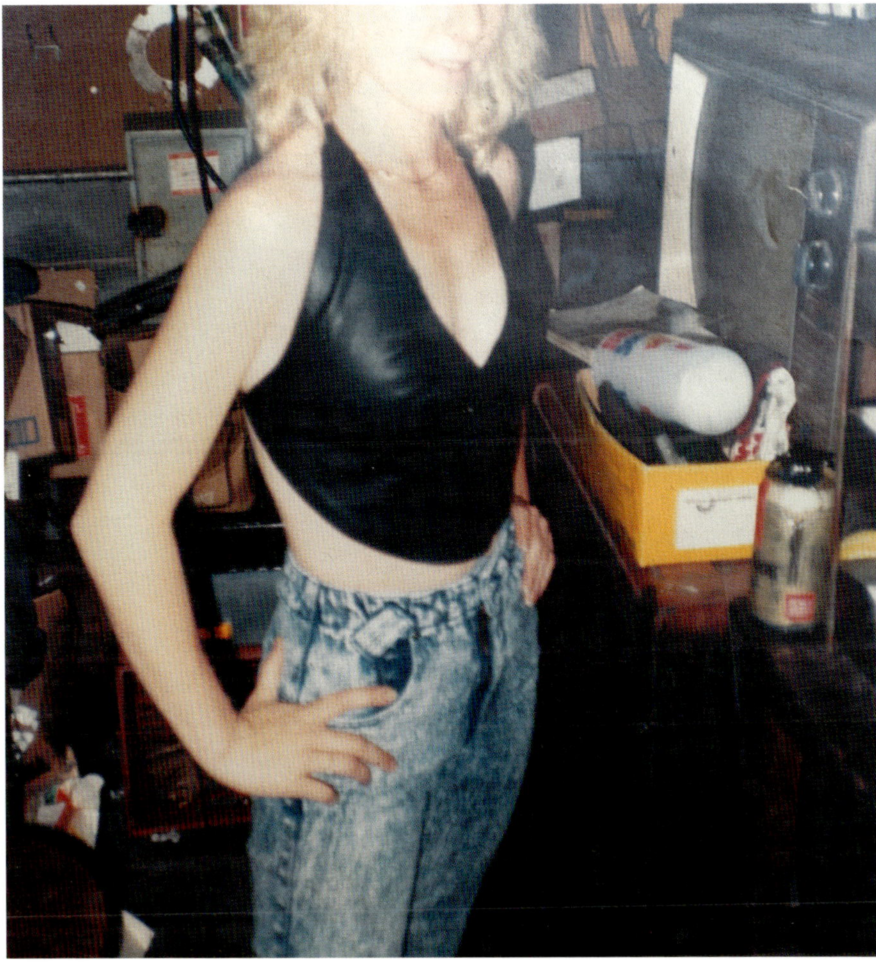

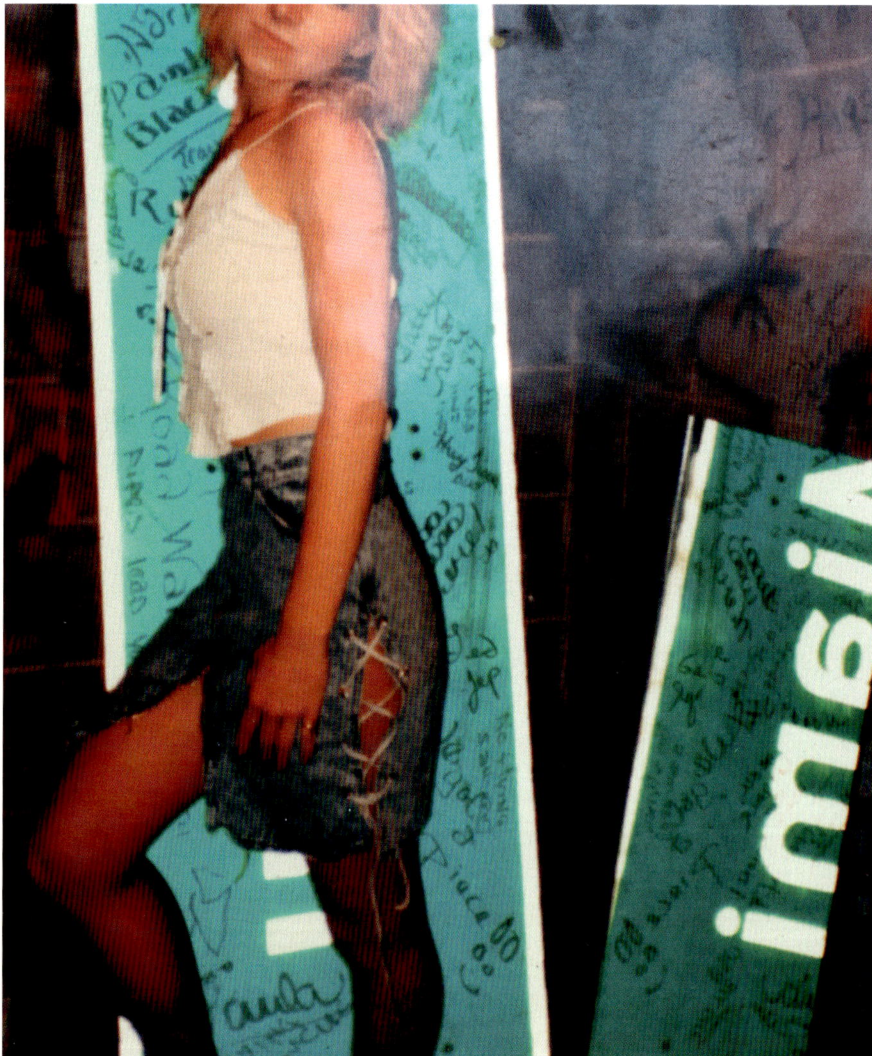

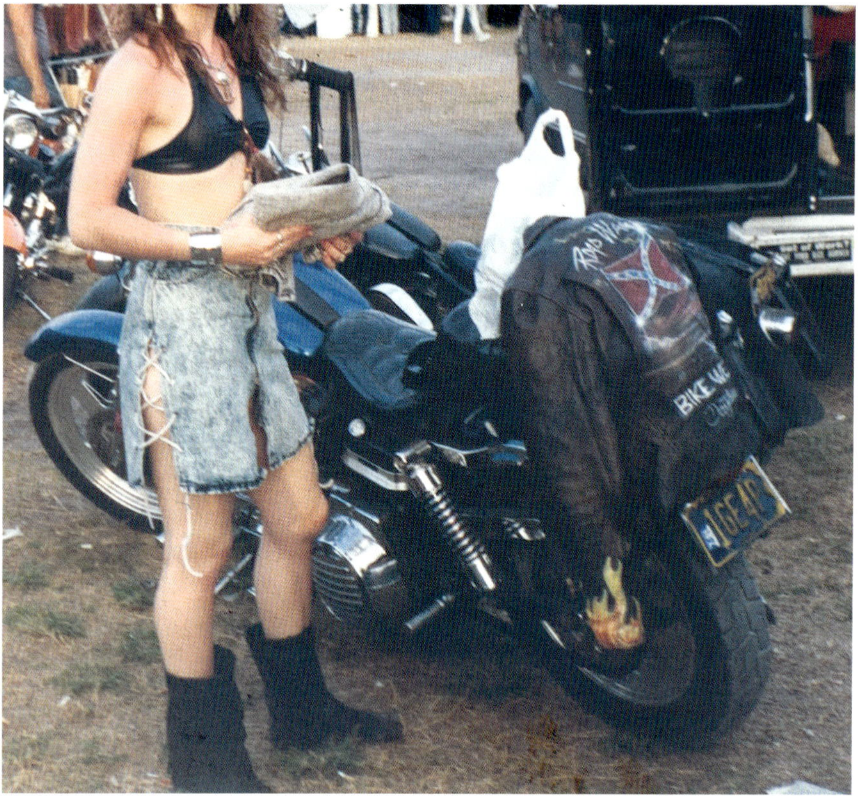

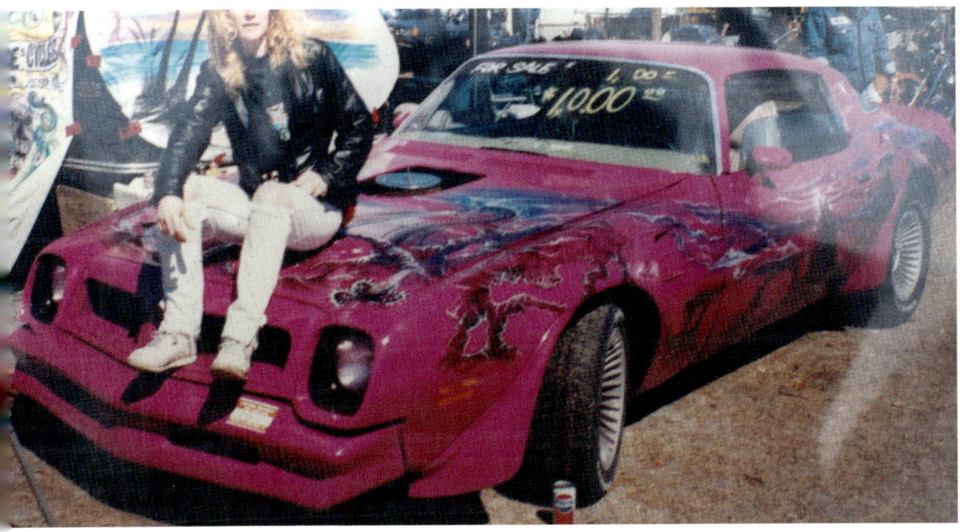
FOR SALE

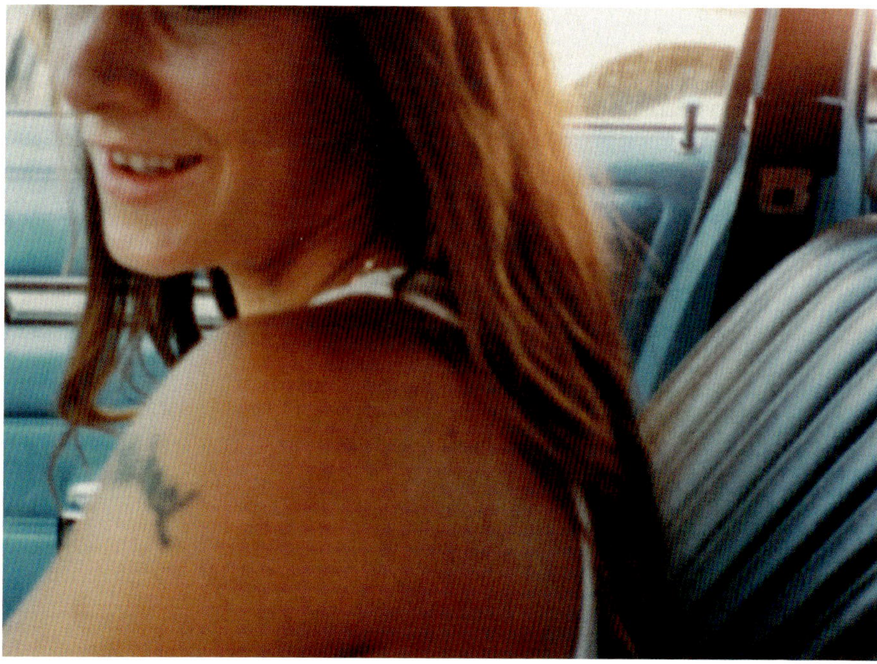

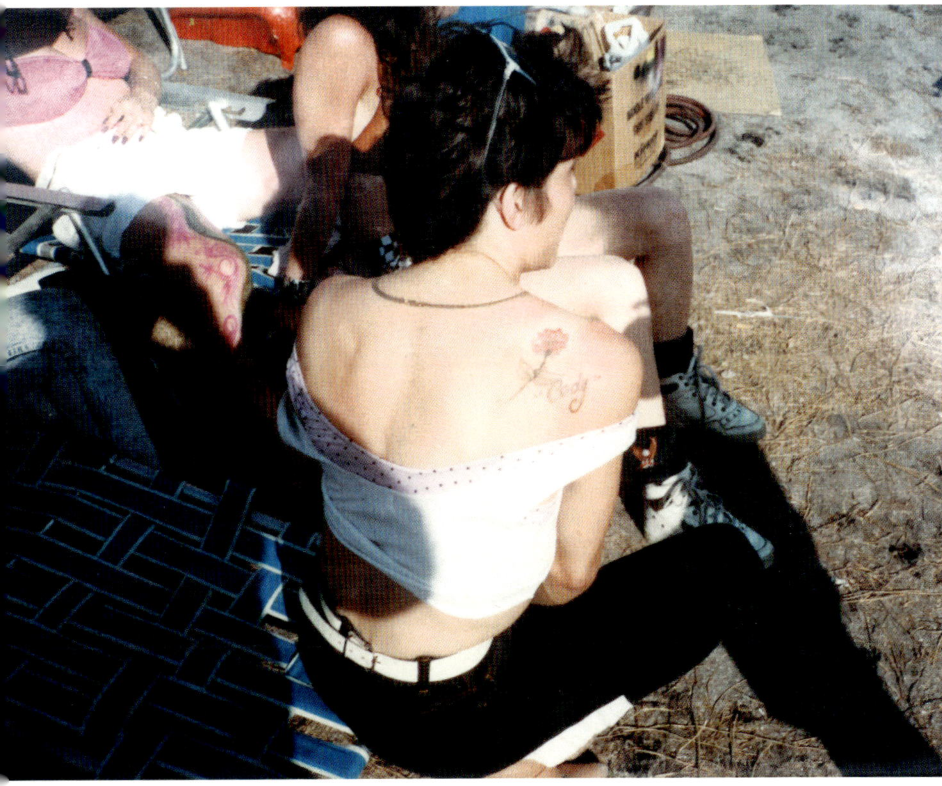

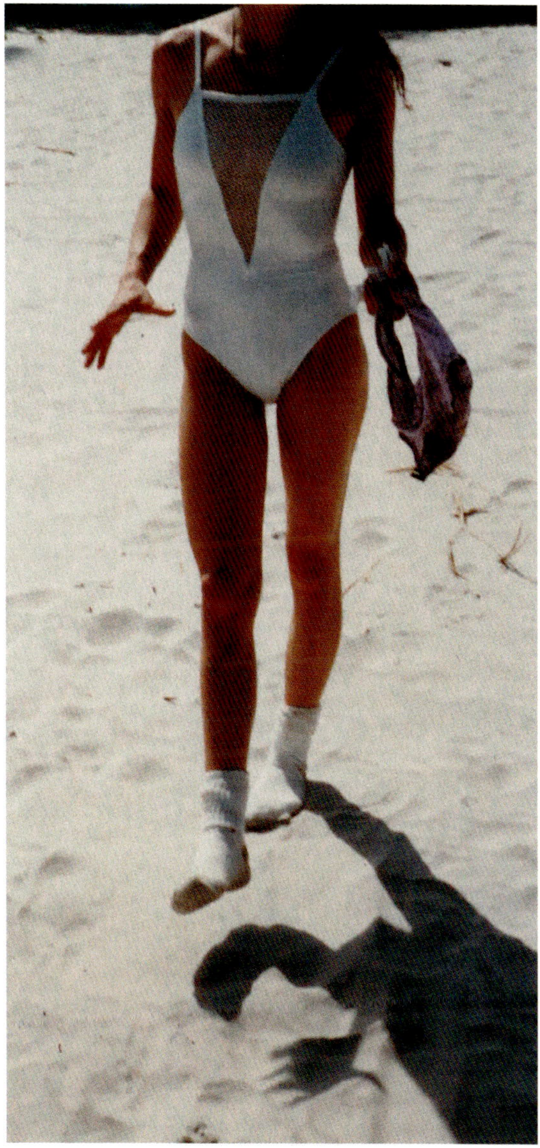

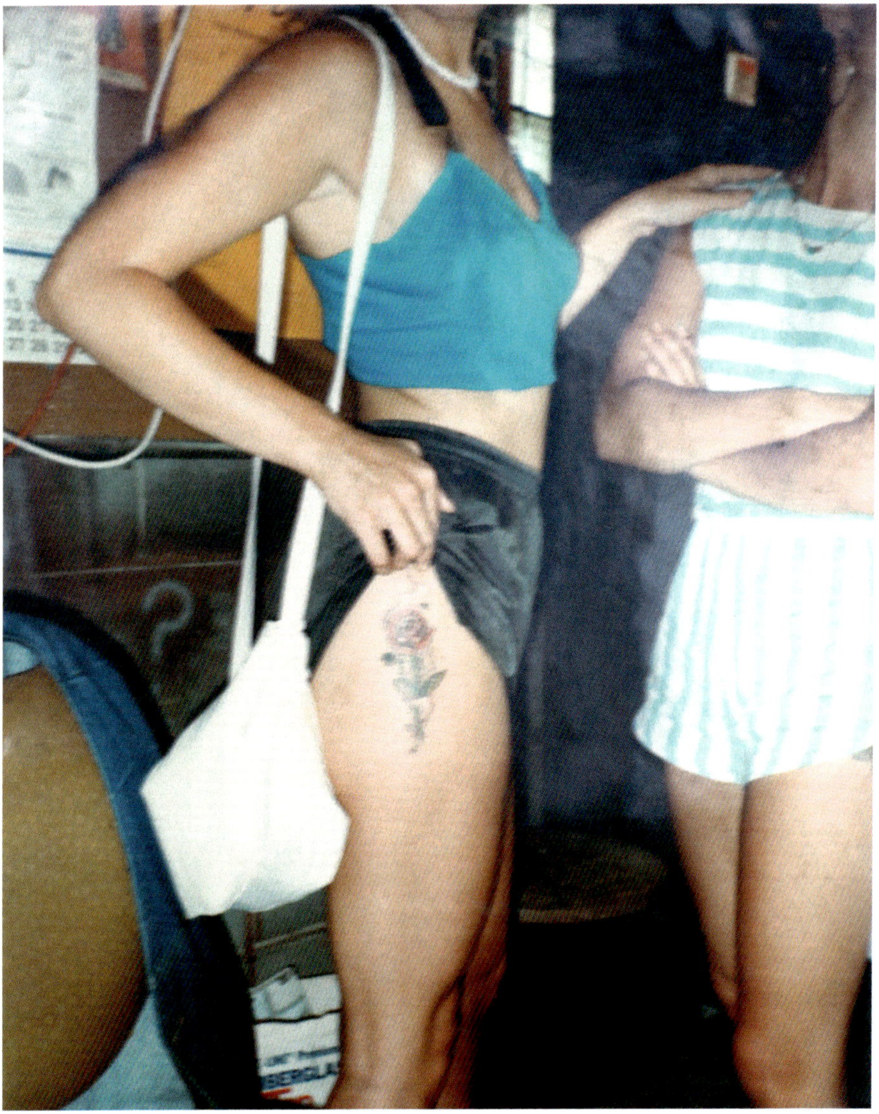

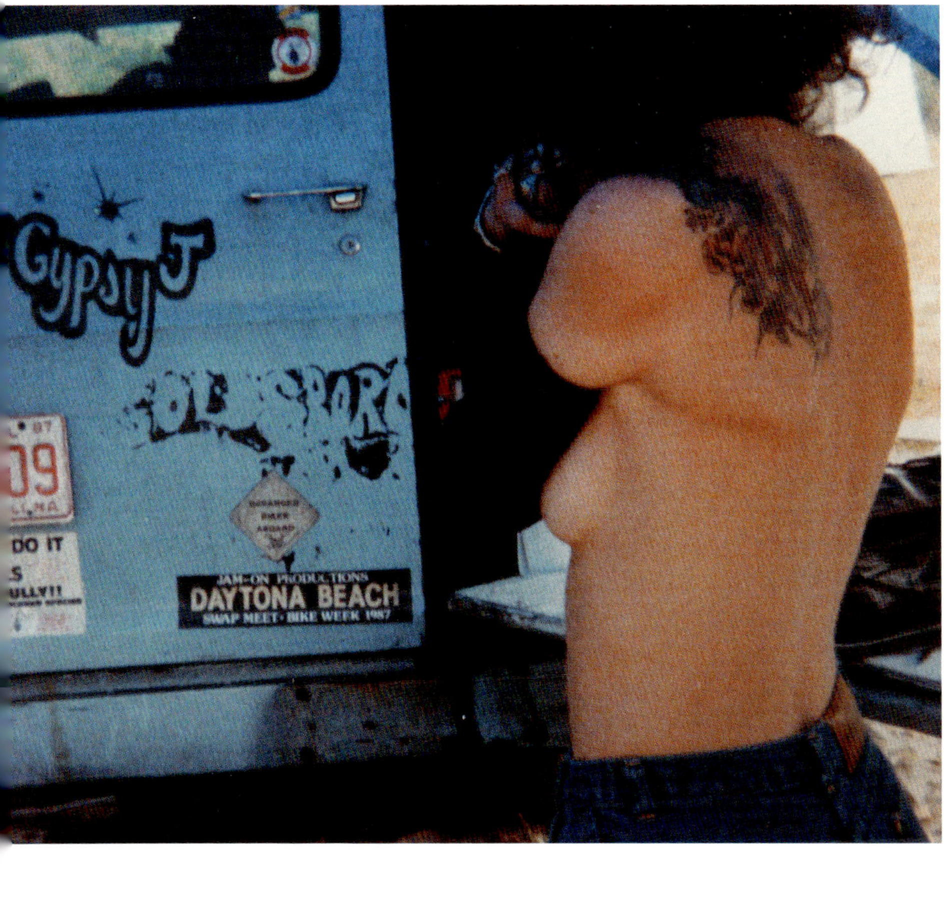
Gypsy J
JAM-ON PRODUCTIONS
DAYTONA BEACH
SWAP MEET · BIKE WEEK 1987

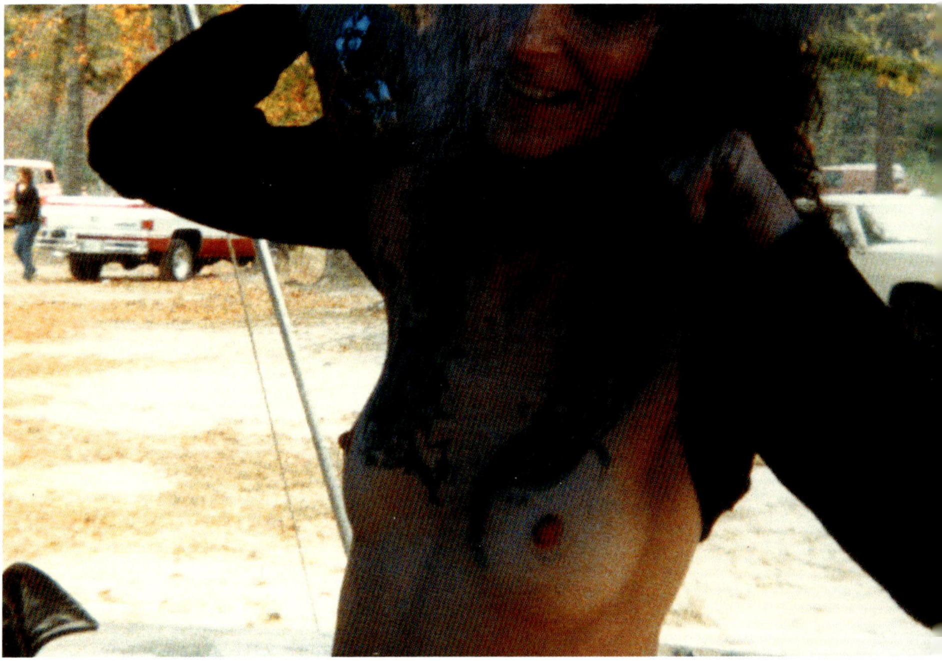

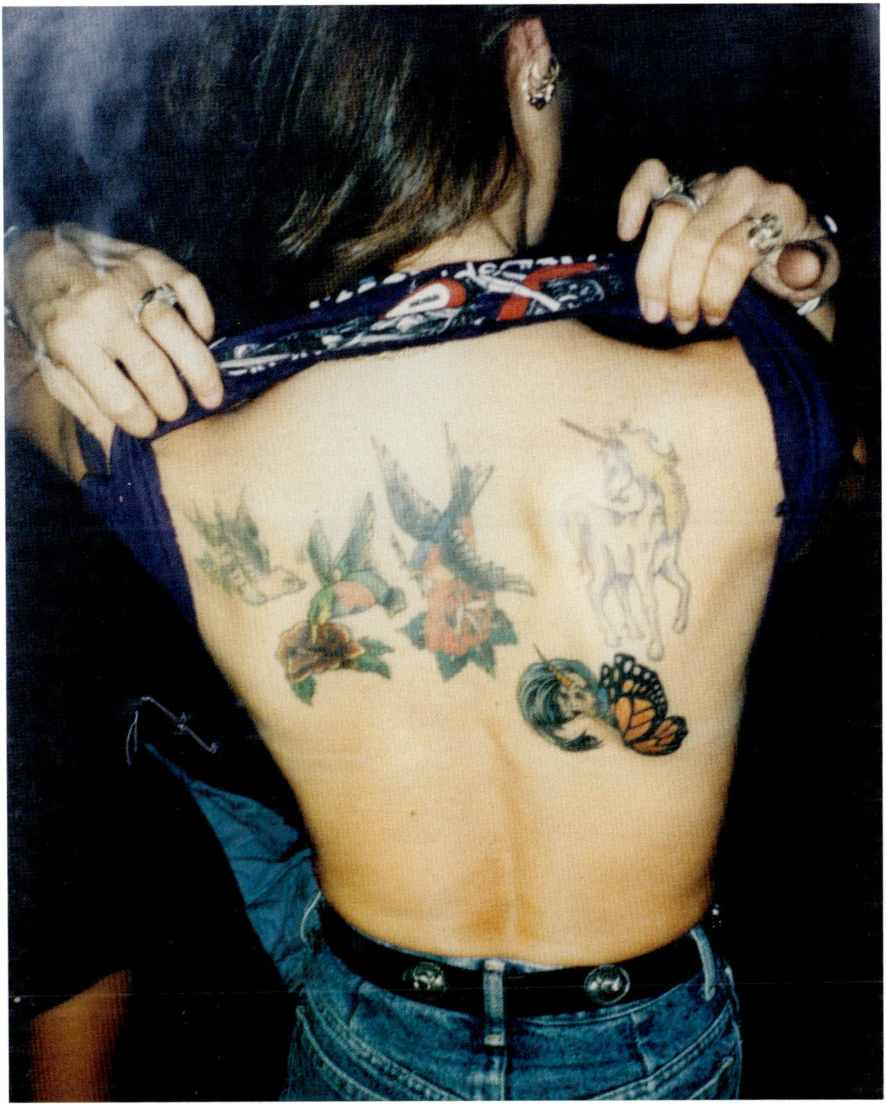

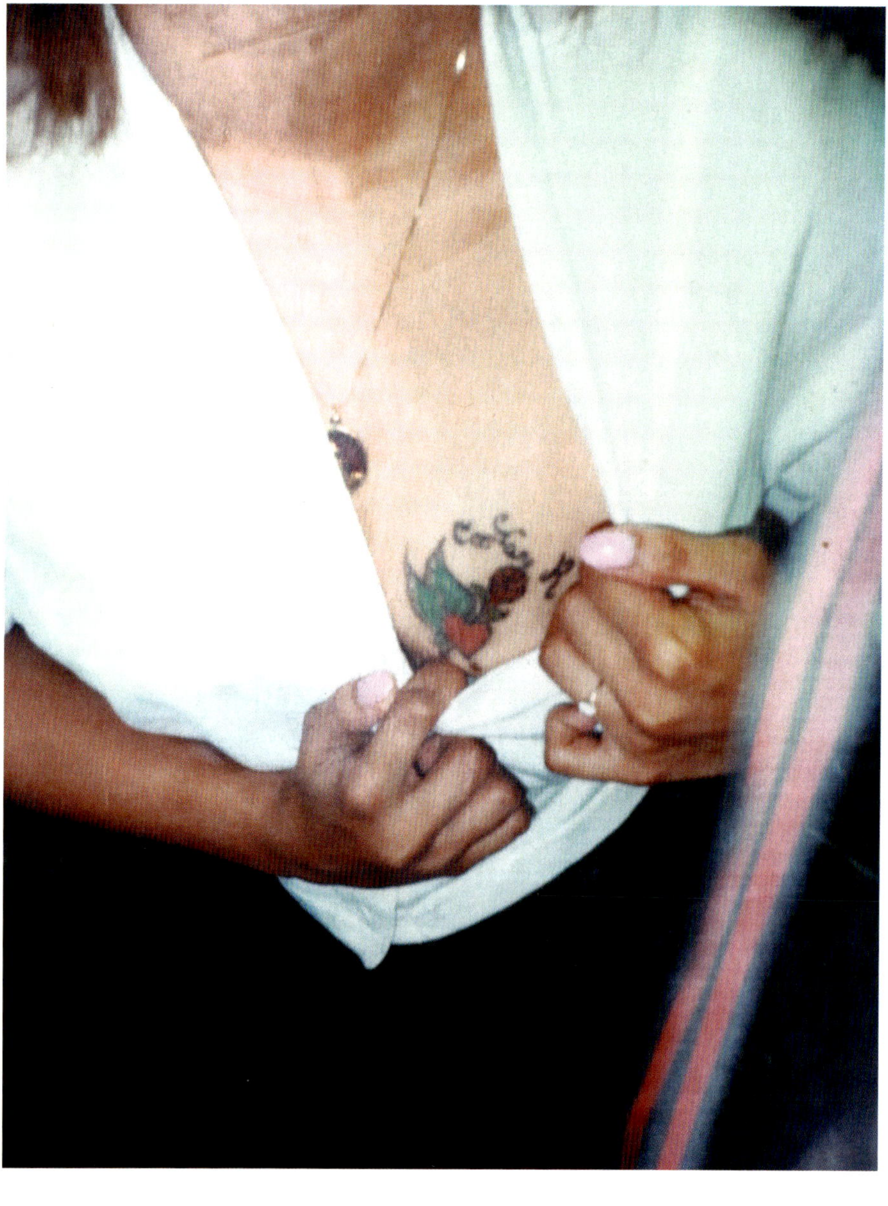

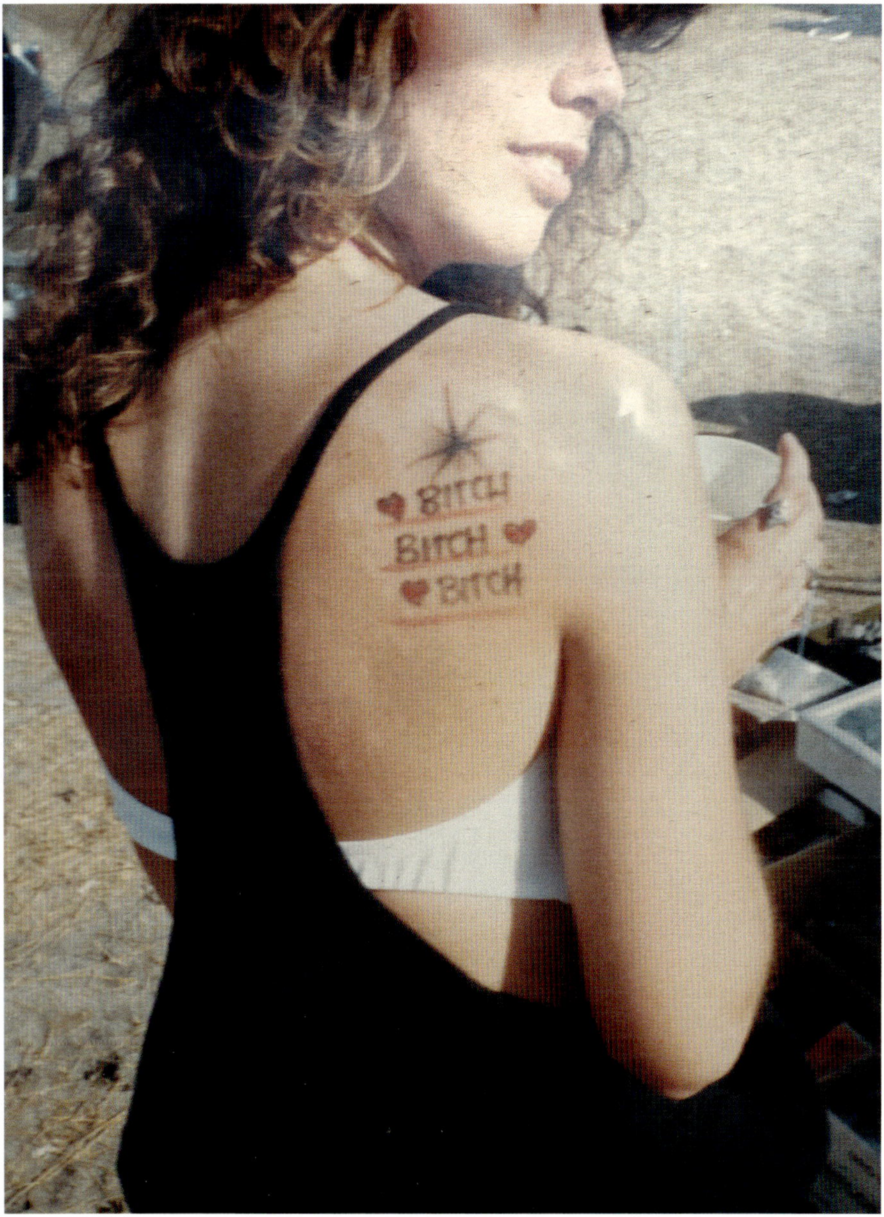
BITCH
BITCH
BITCH

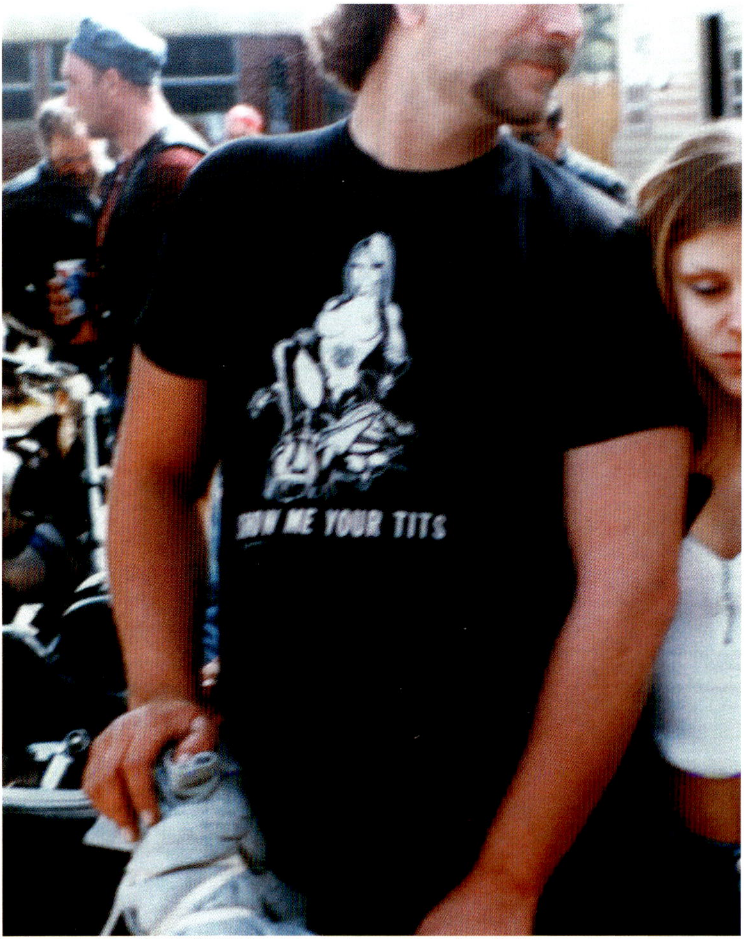
ME YOUR TITS

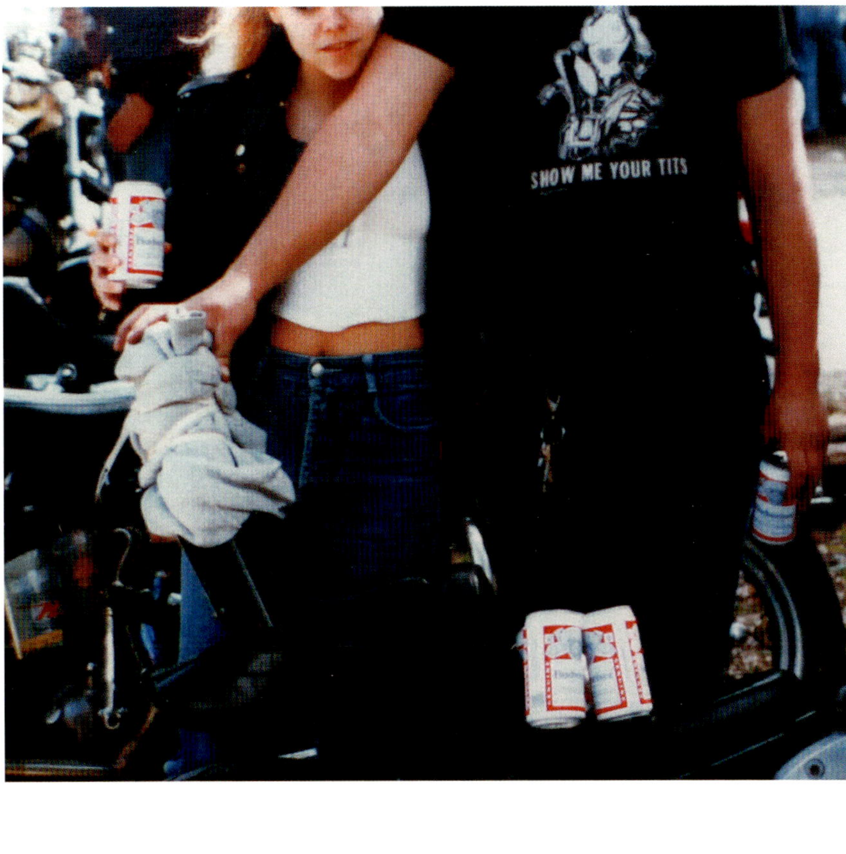
SHOW ME YOUR TITS

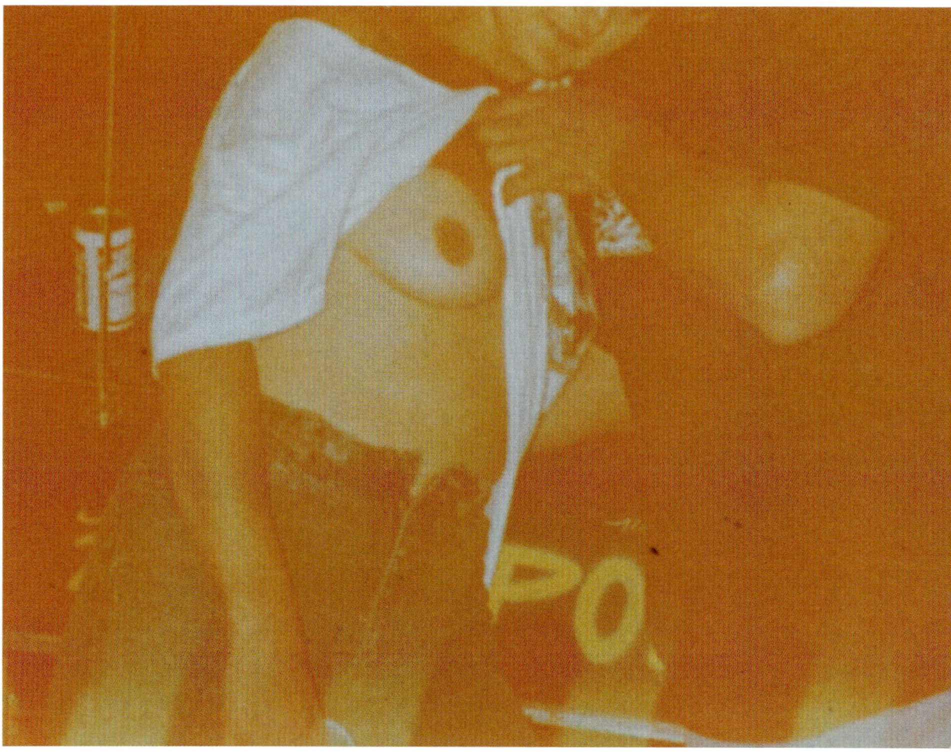
PO

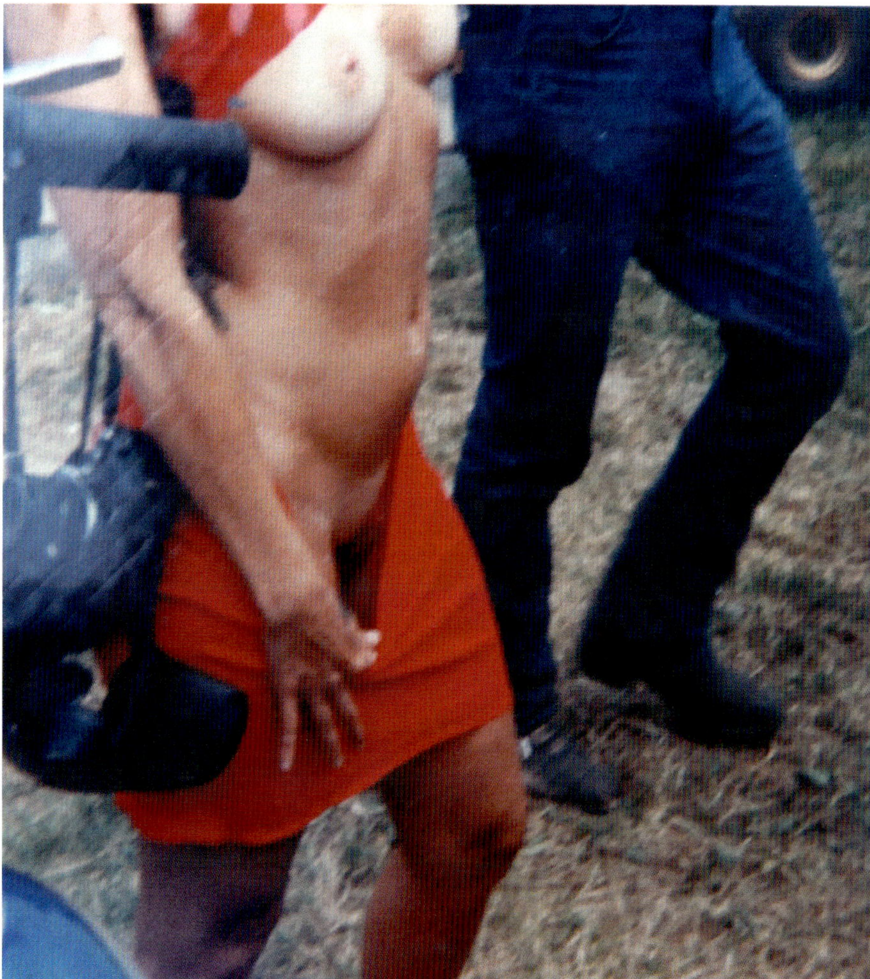

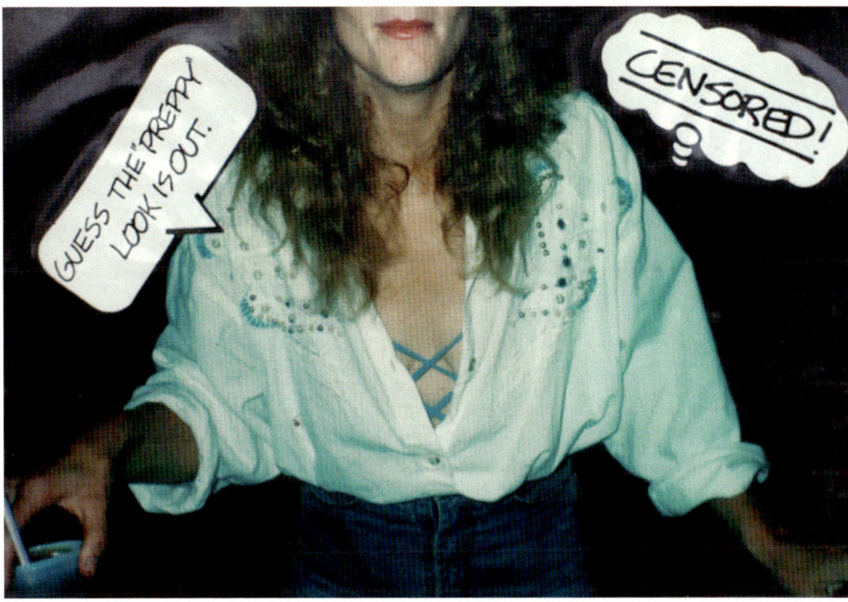
GUESS THE "PREPPY" LOOK IS OUT.
CENSORED!

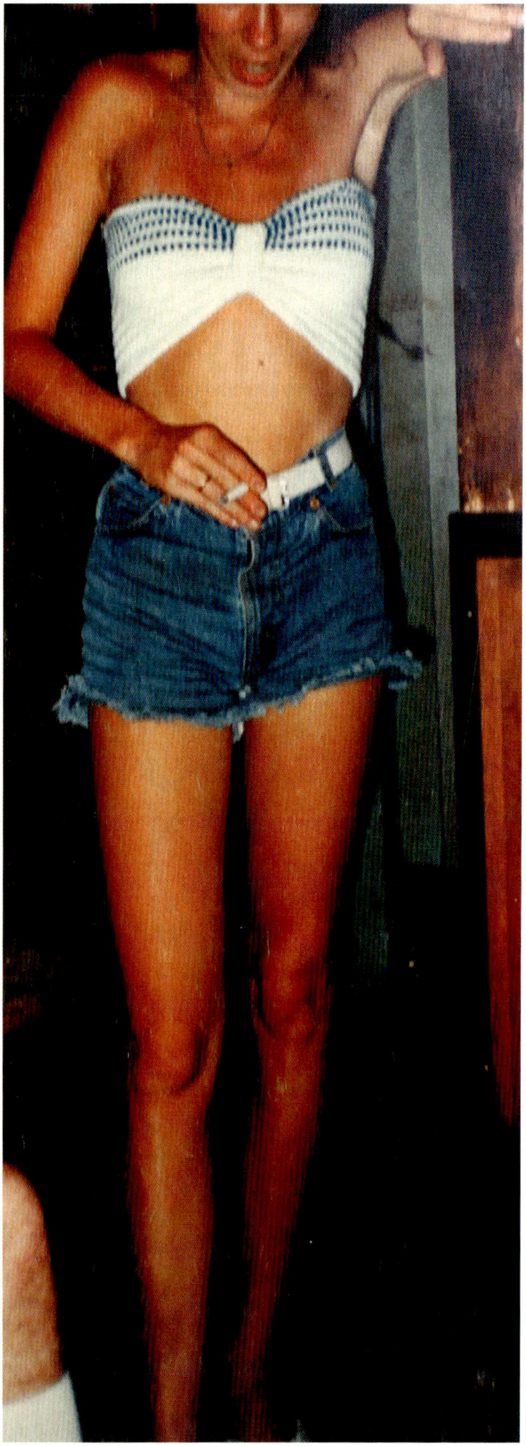

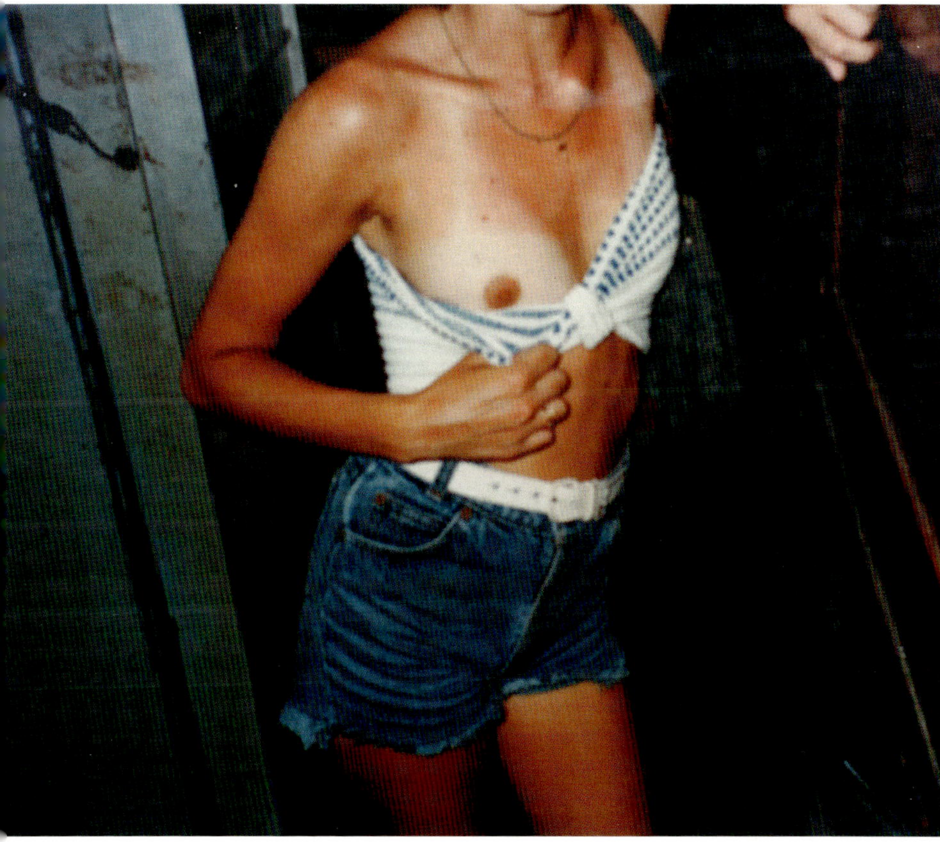

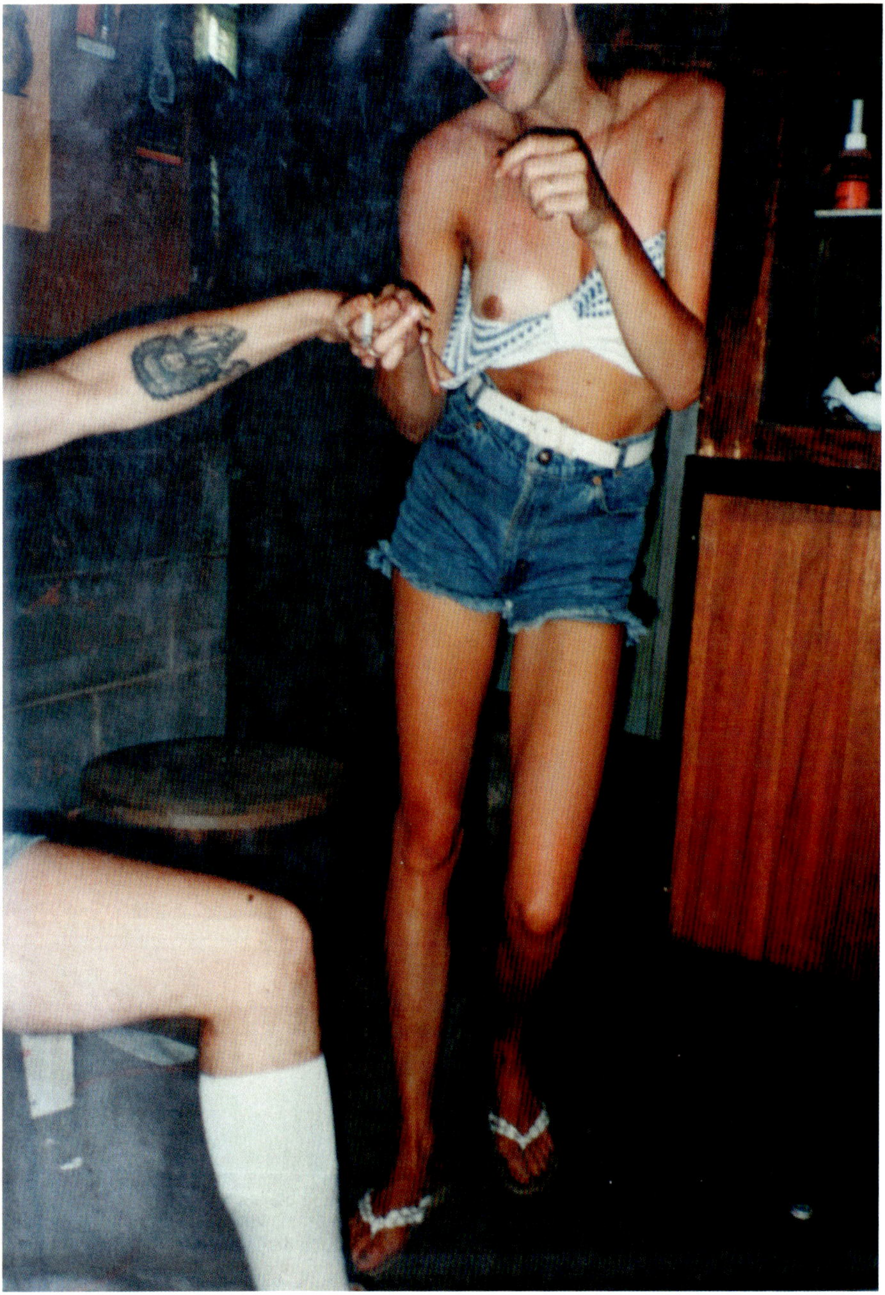

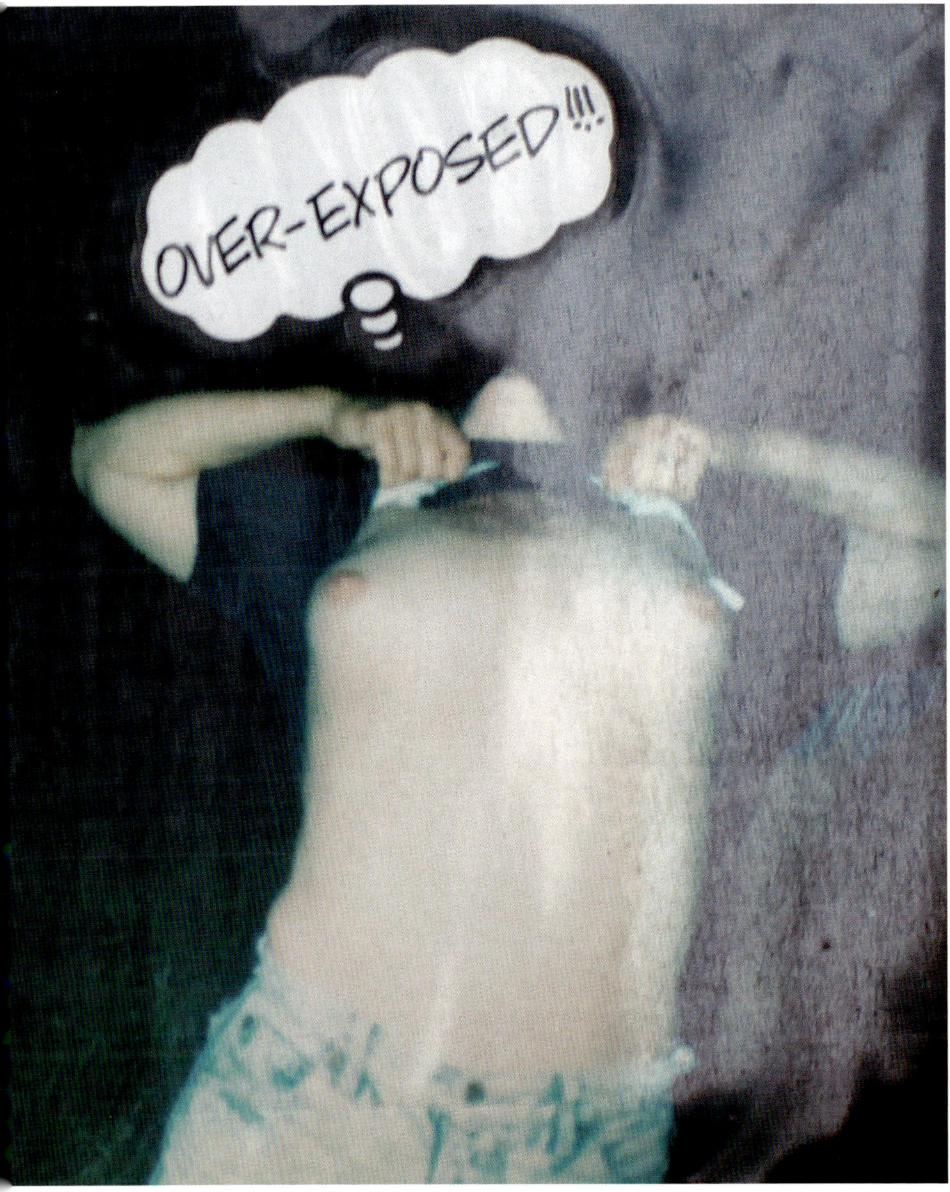
OVER-EXPOSED!!!

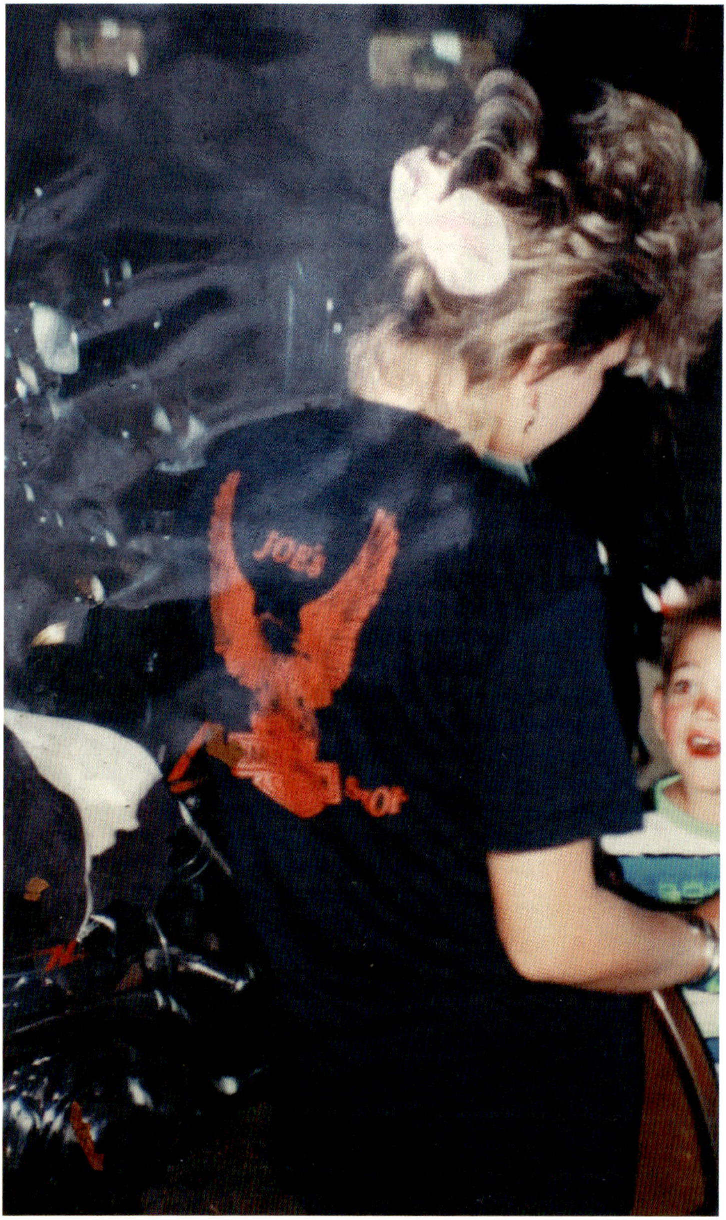
JOE'S

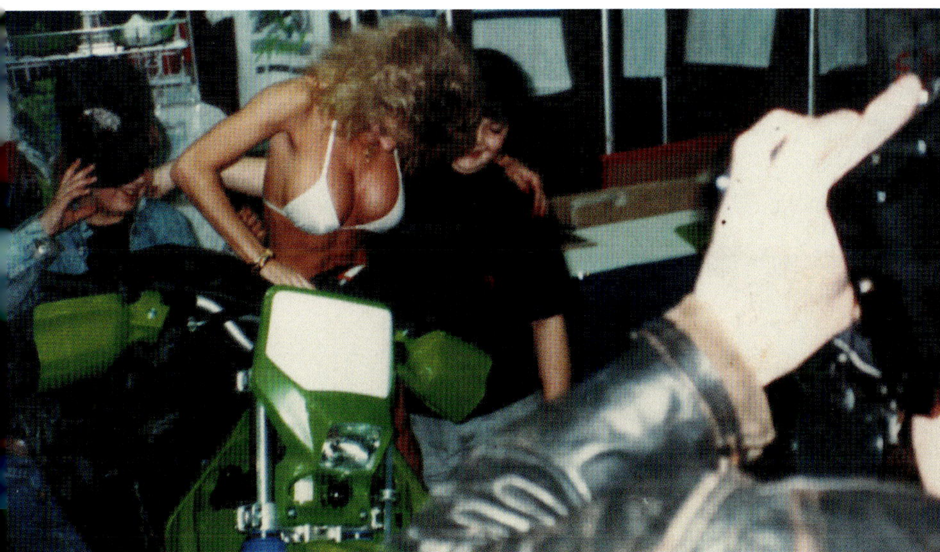

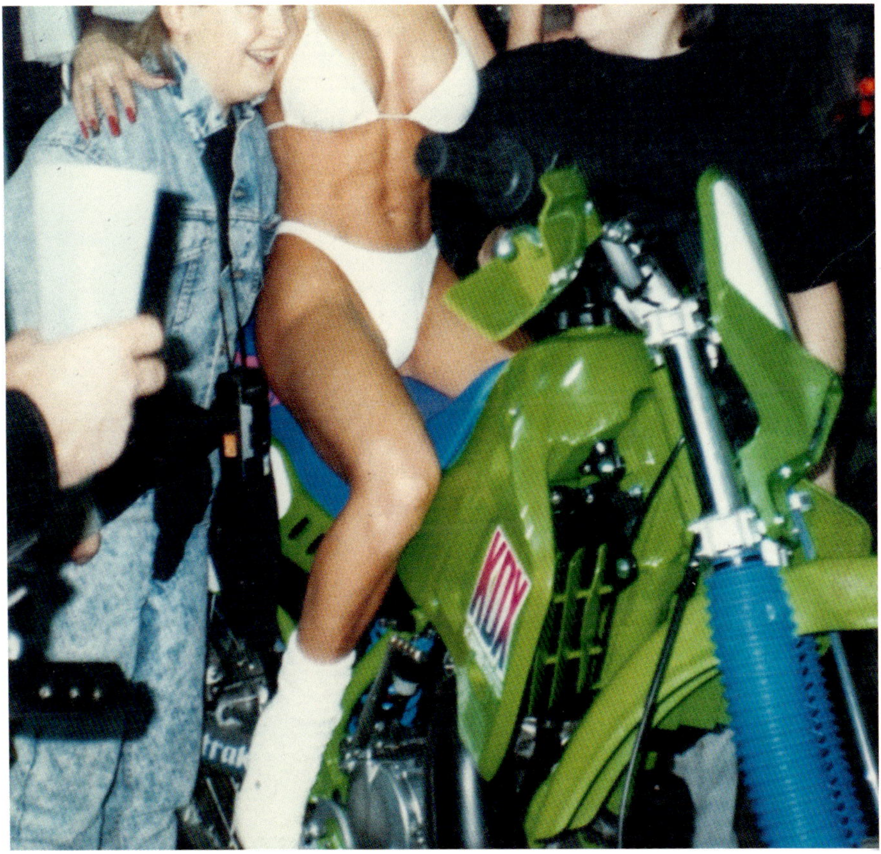
KDX

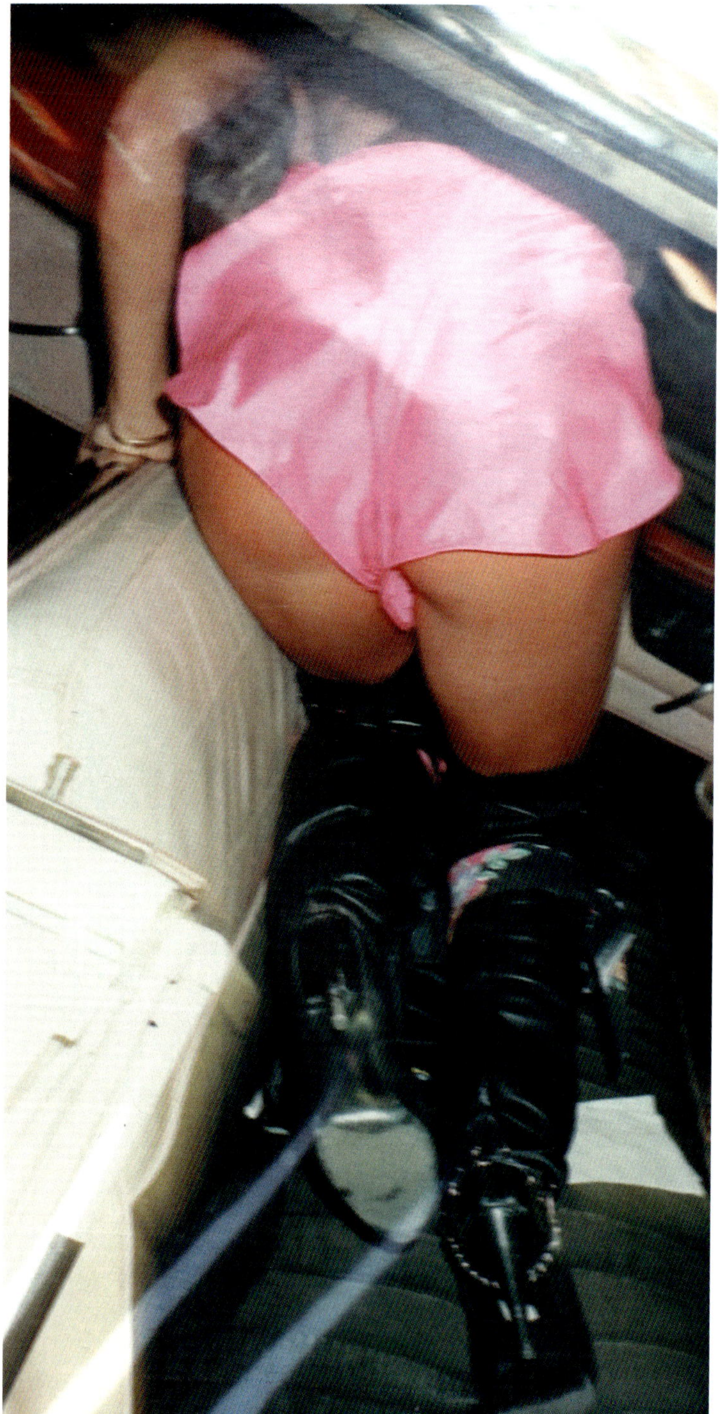

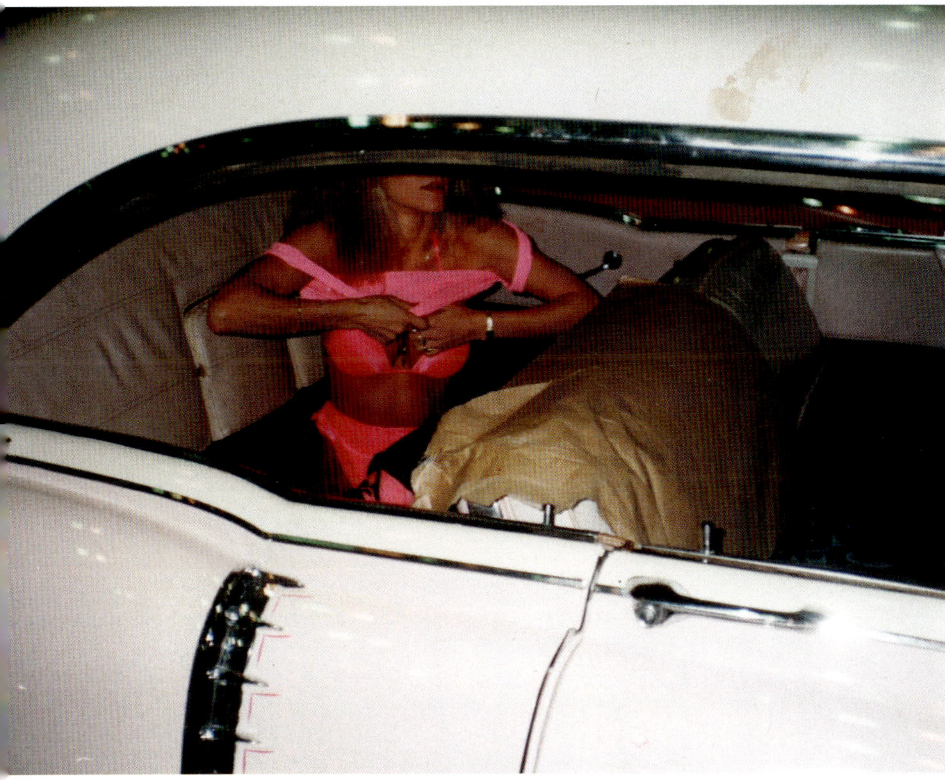

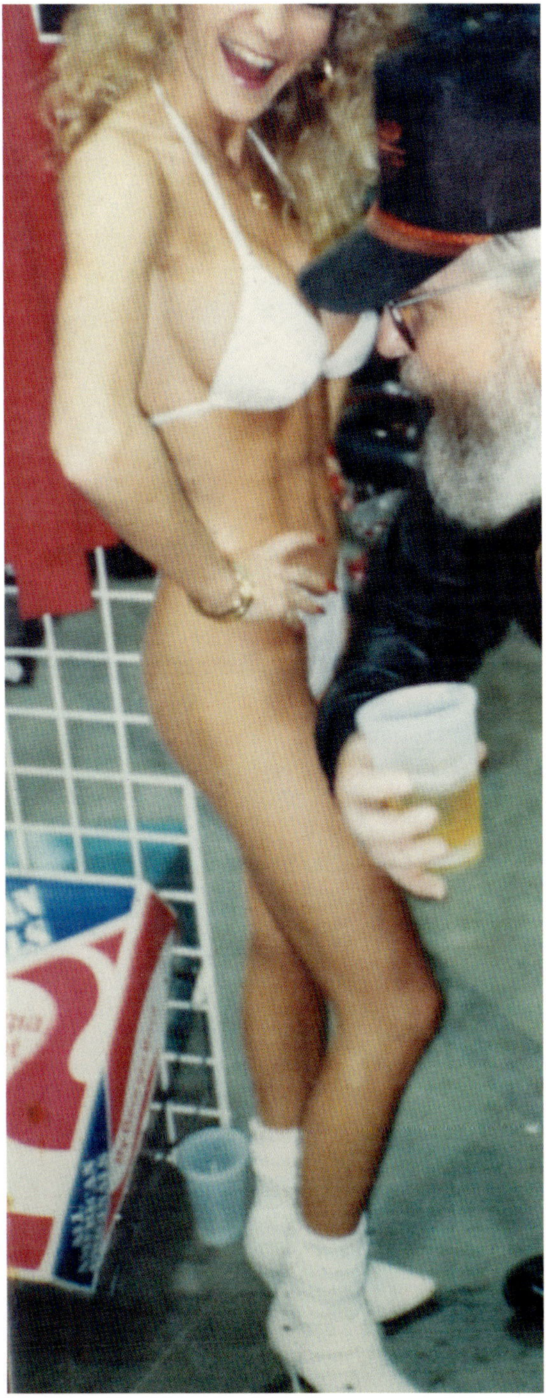

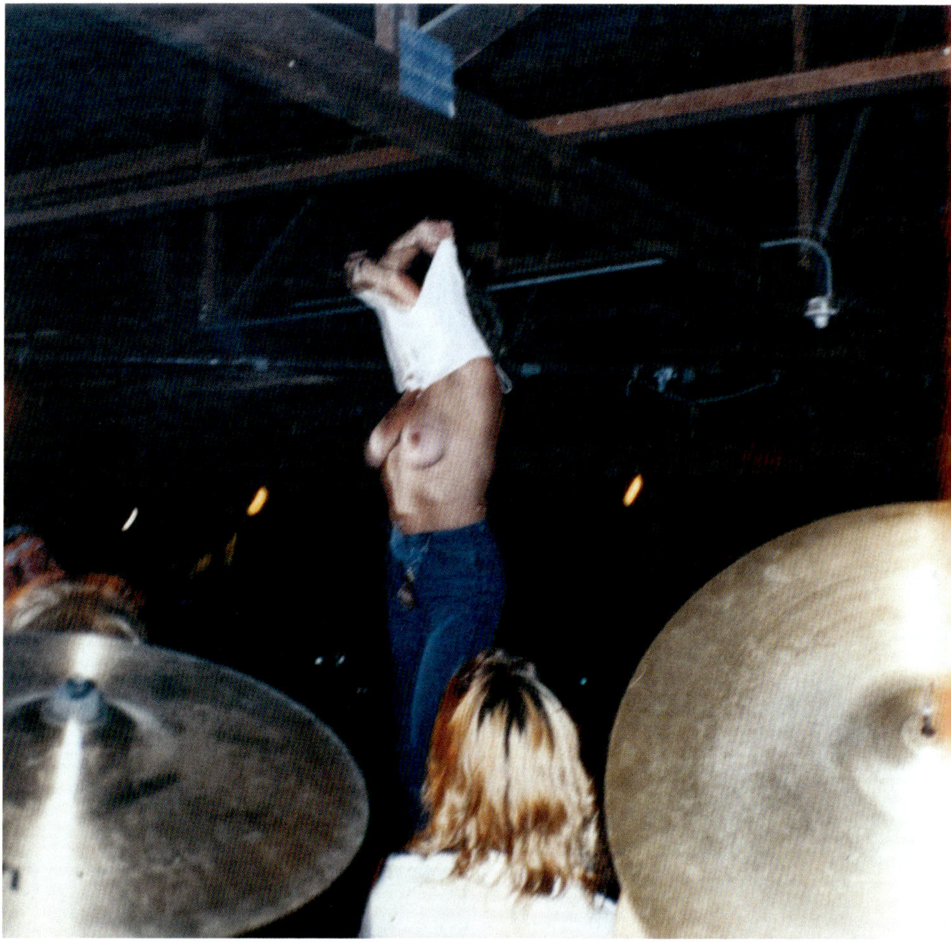

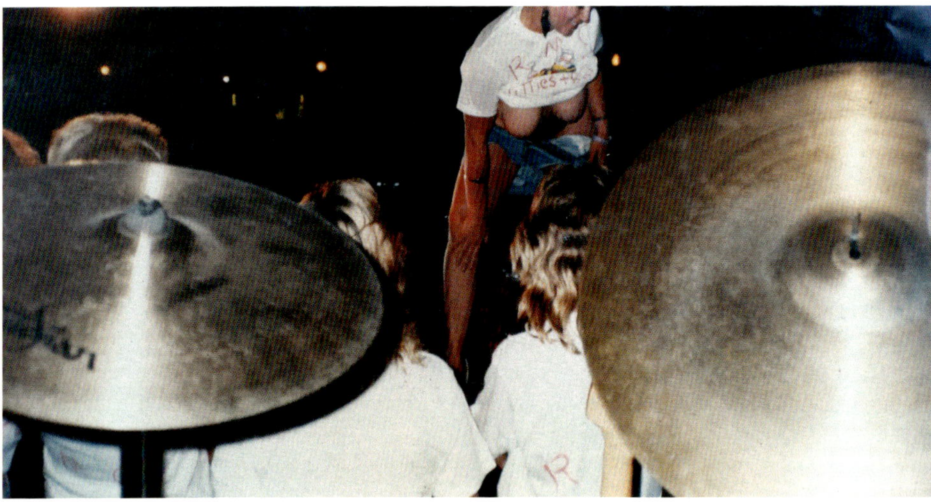

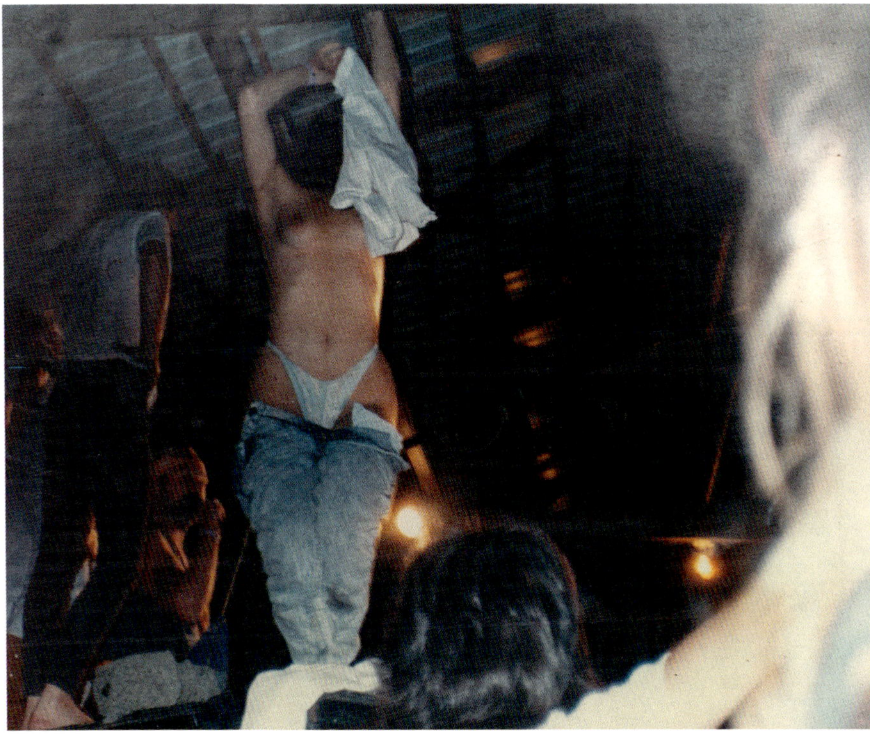

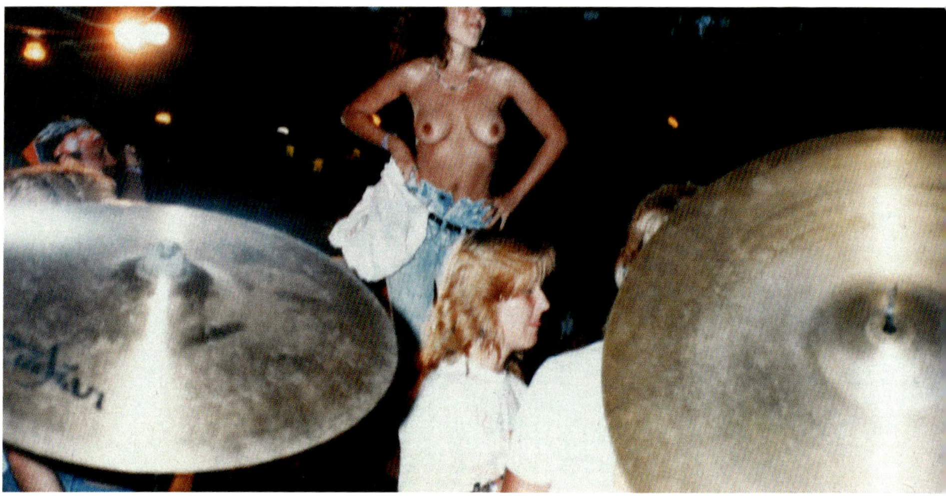

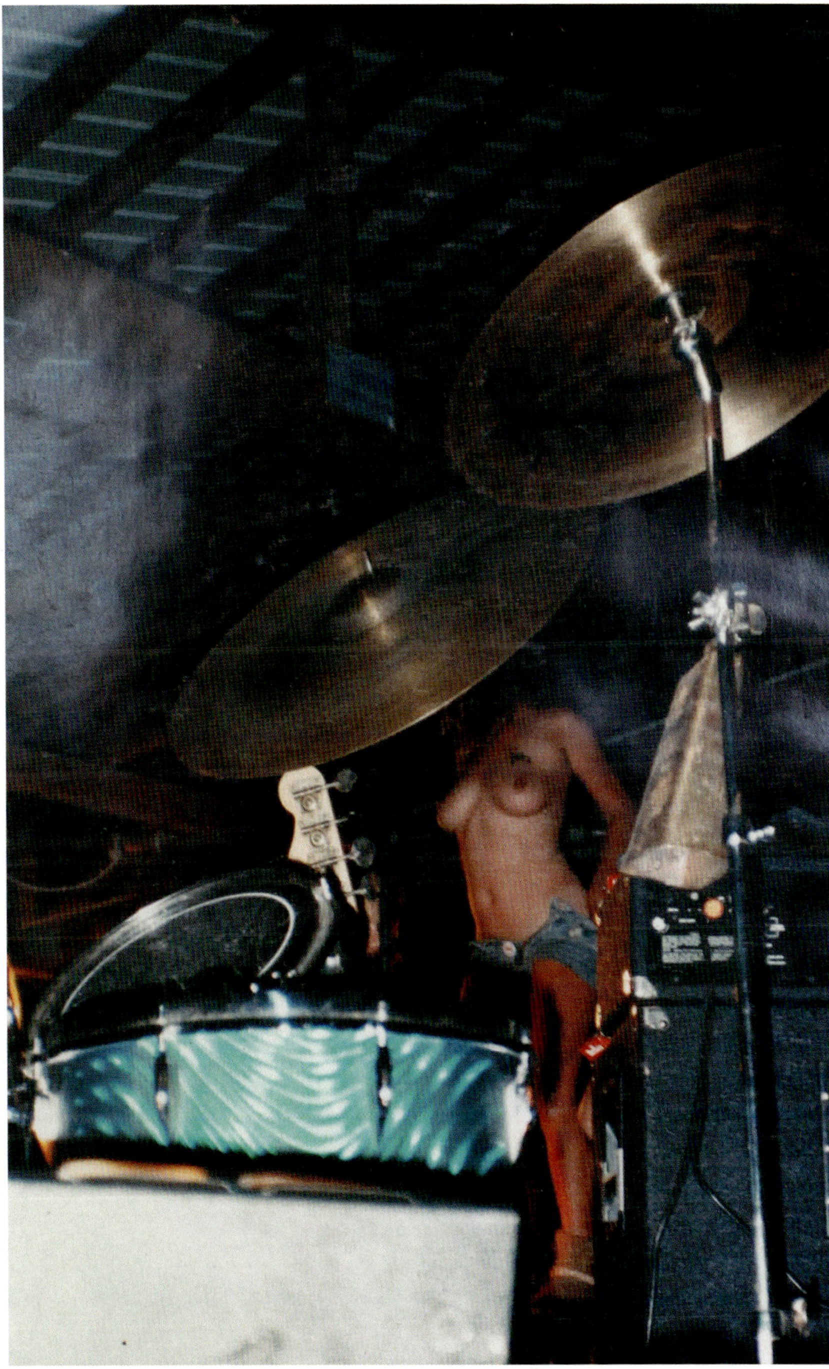

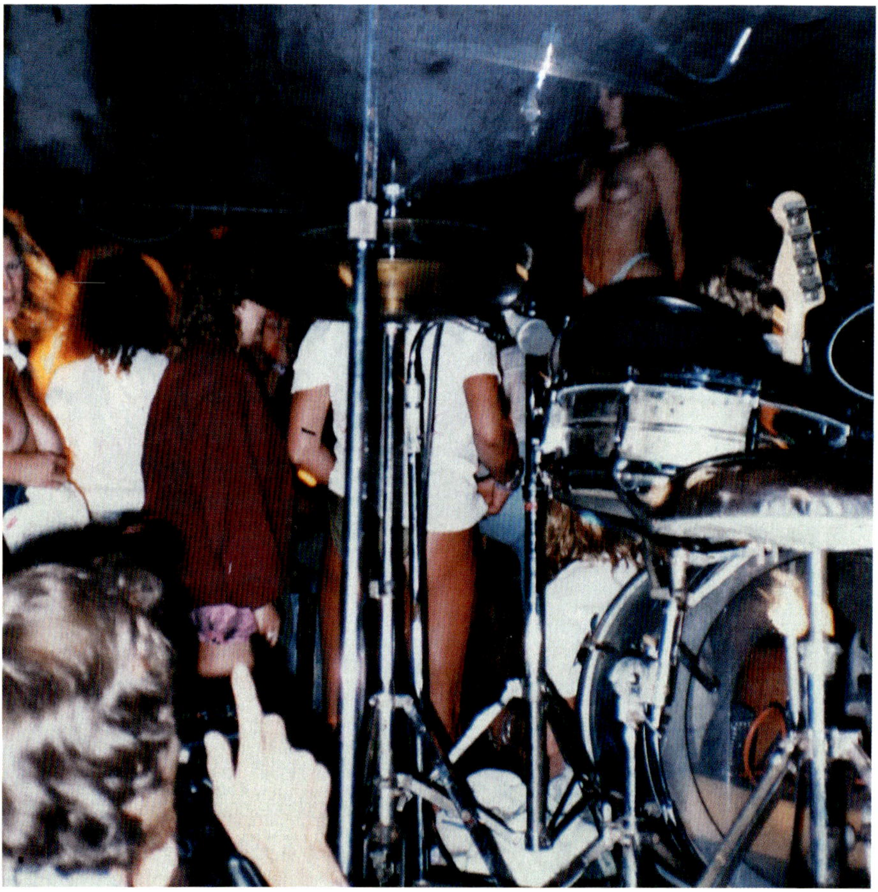

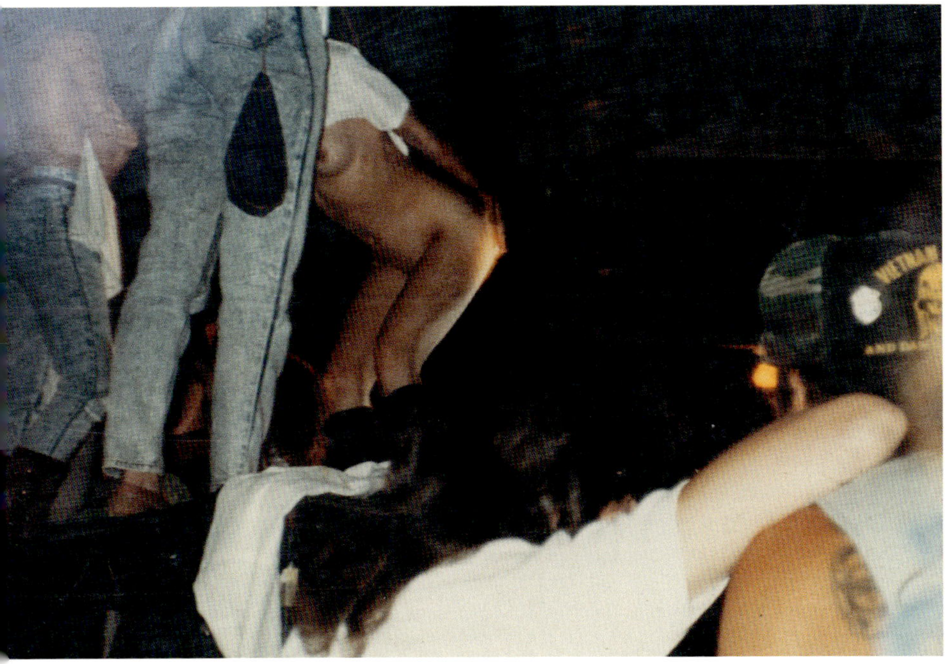

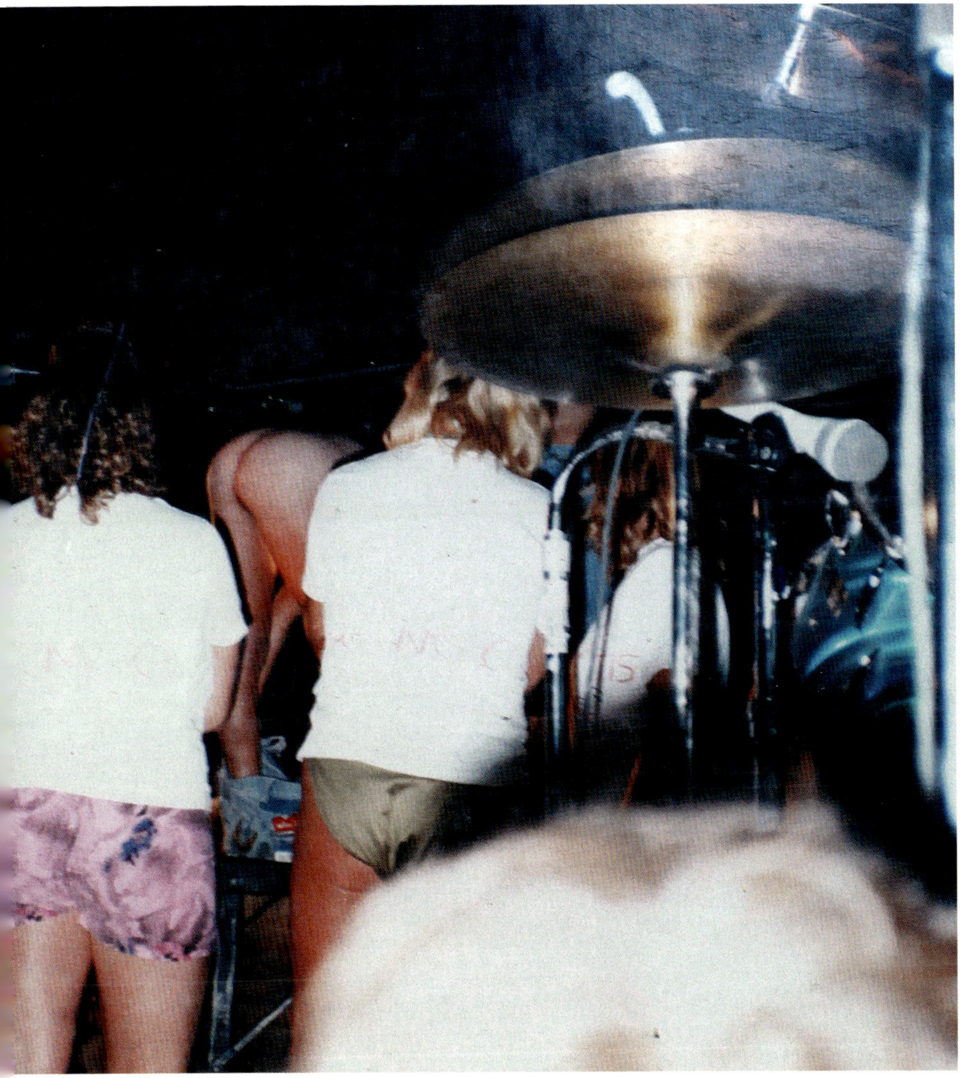

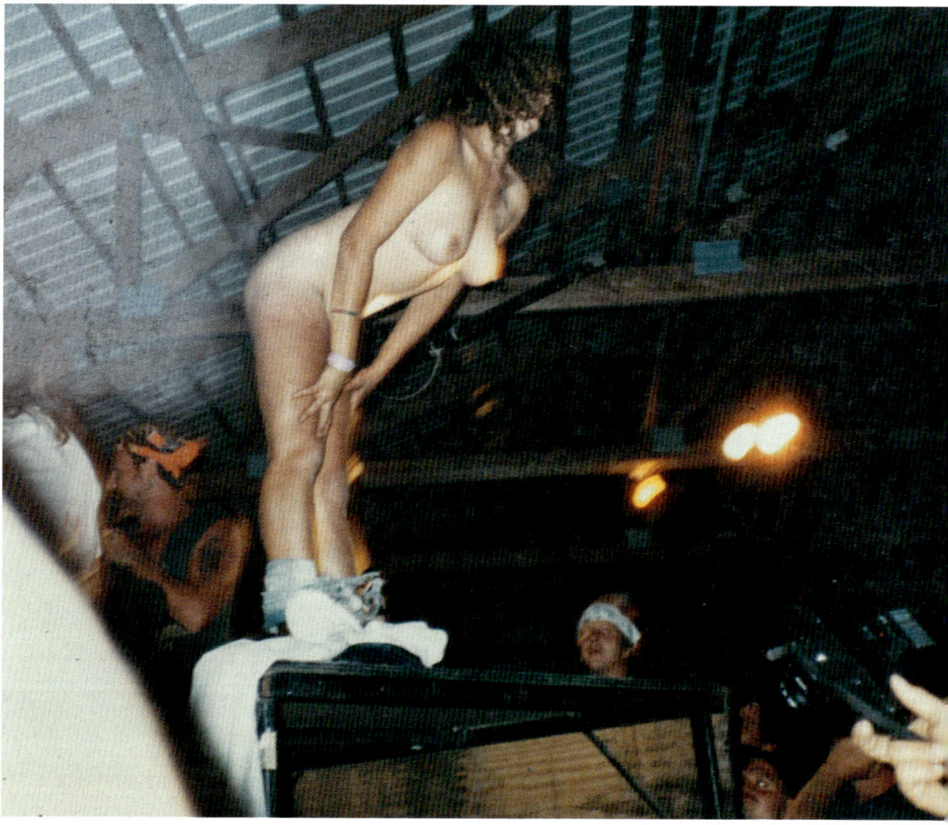

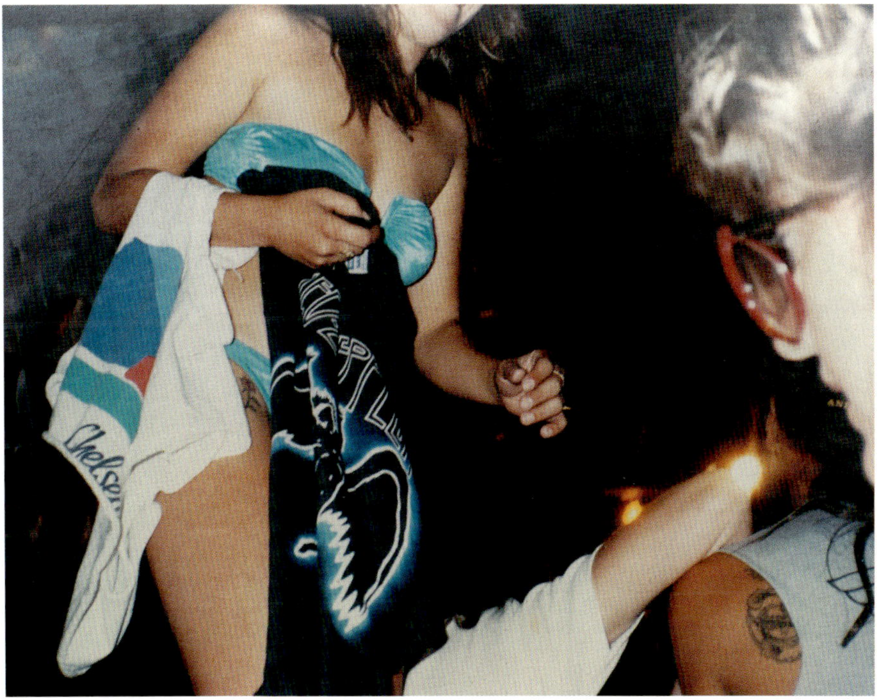

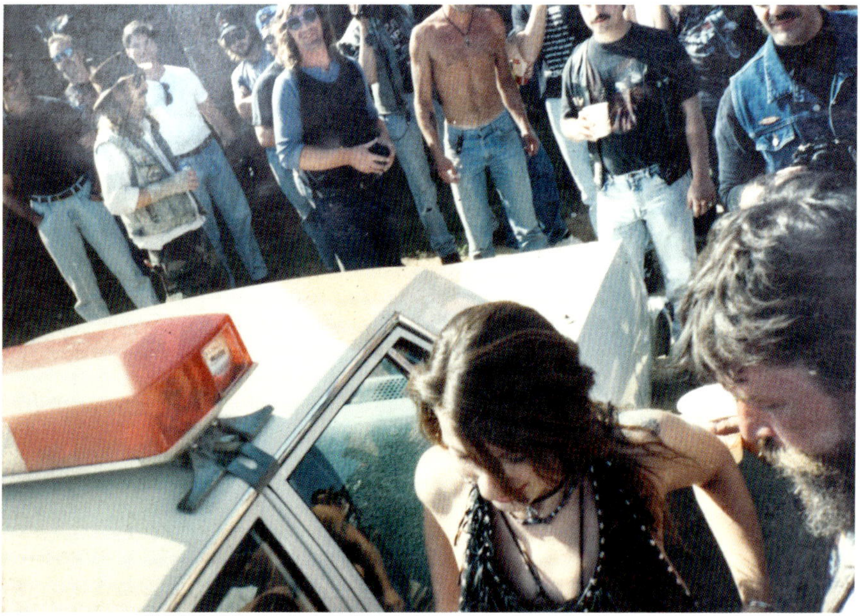

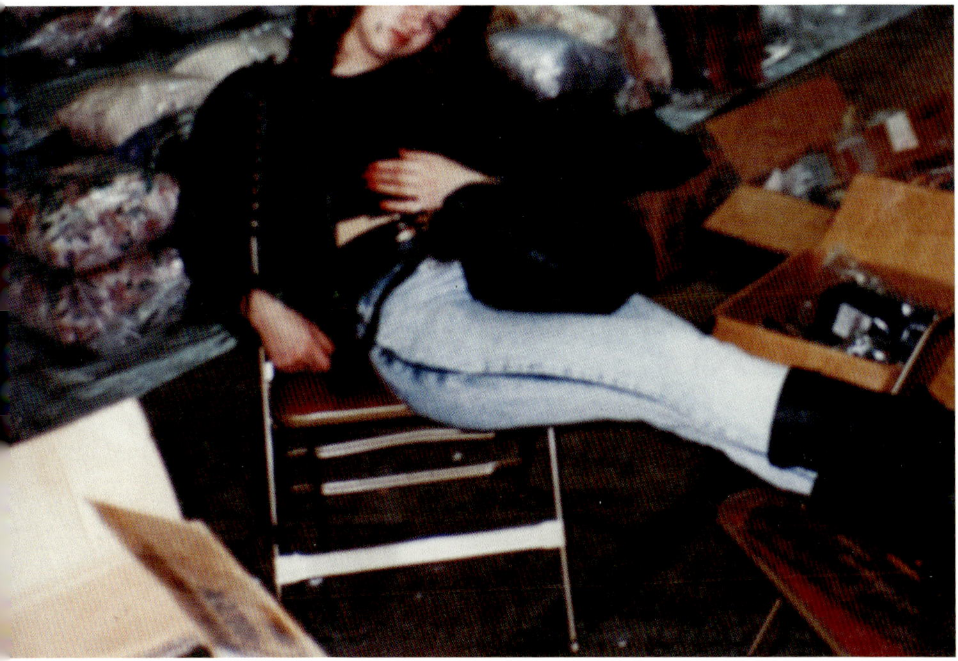

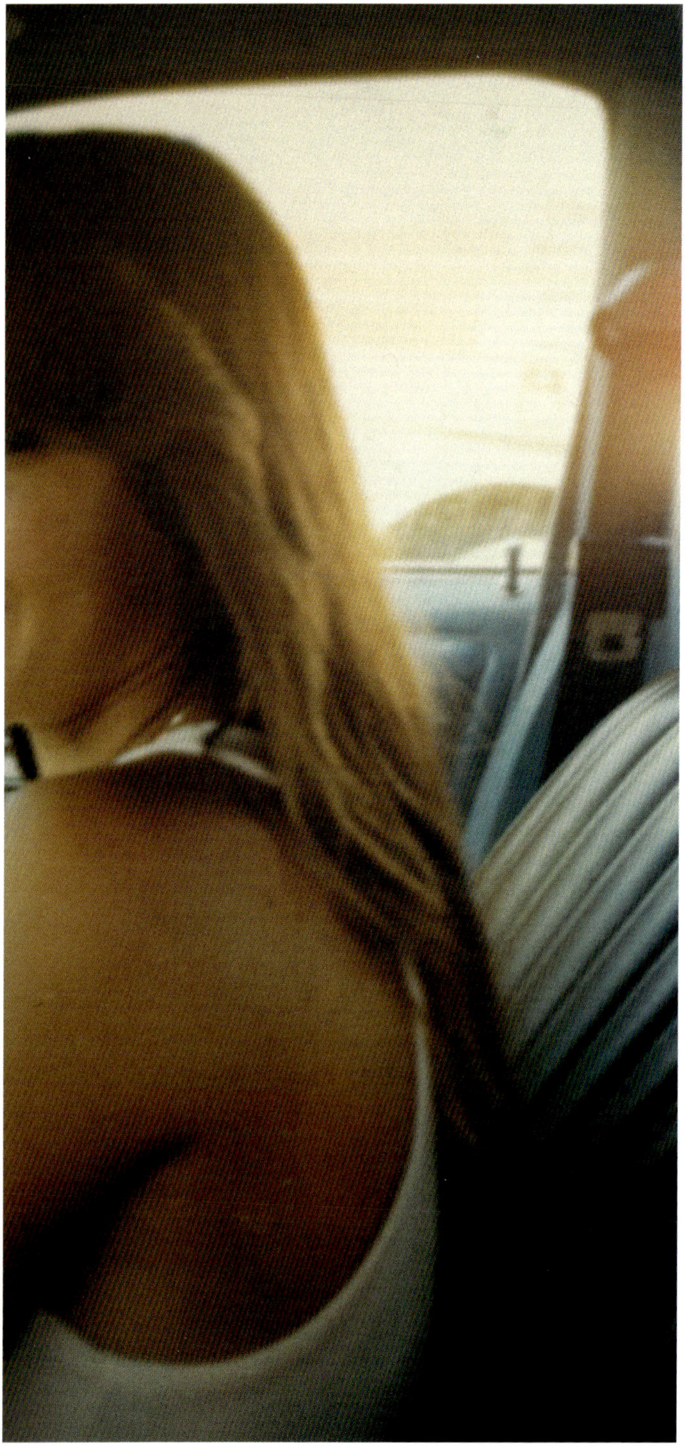

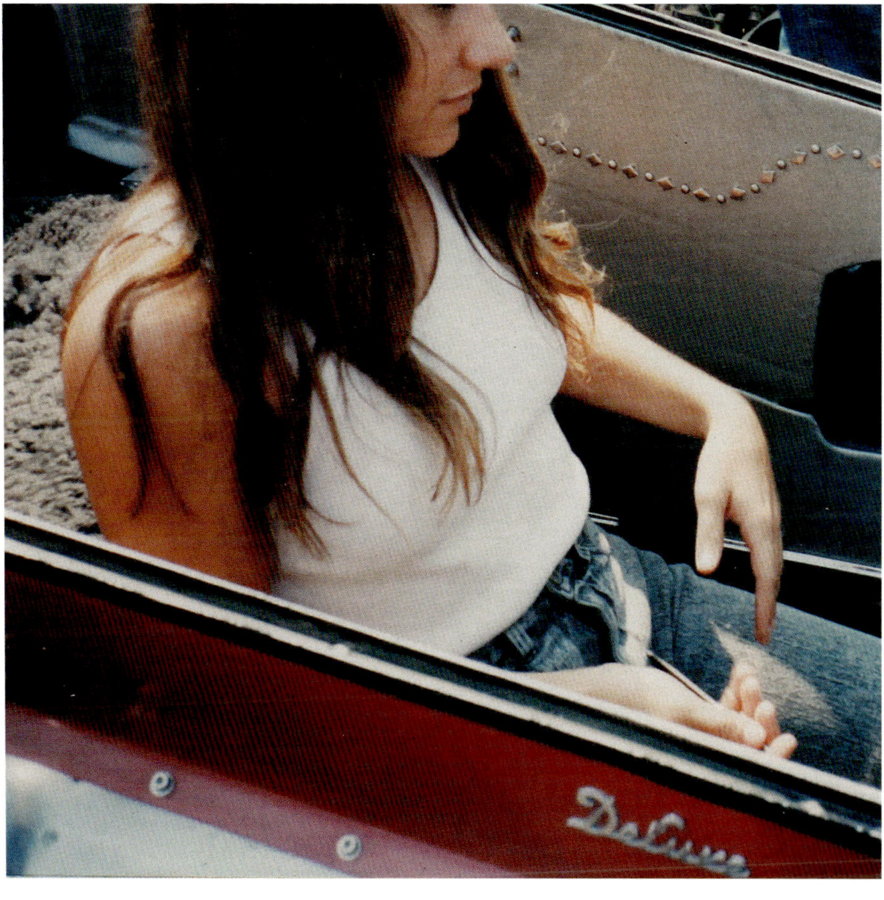

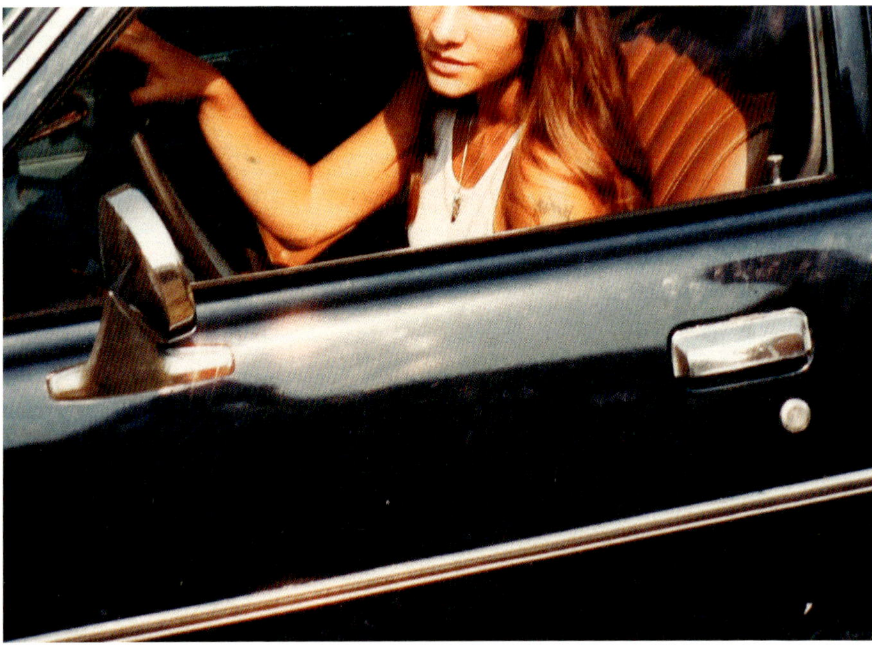

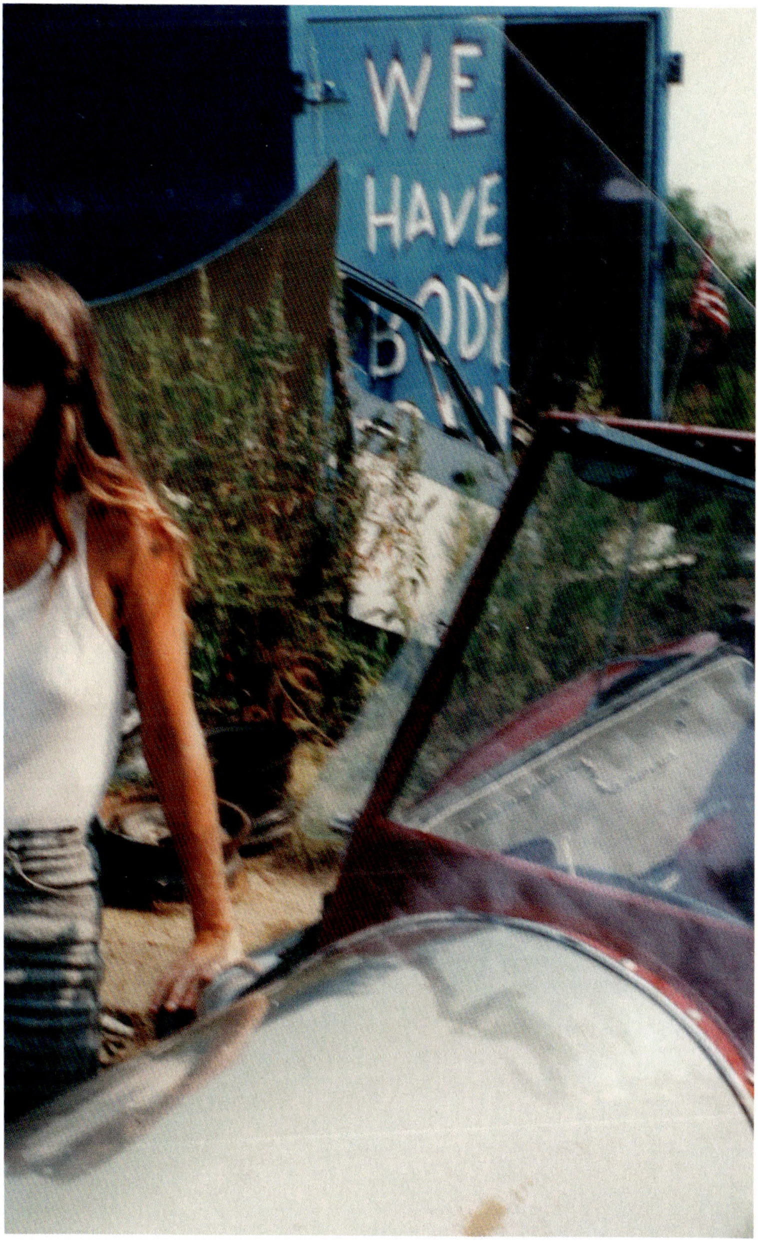
WE
HAVE

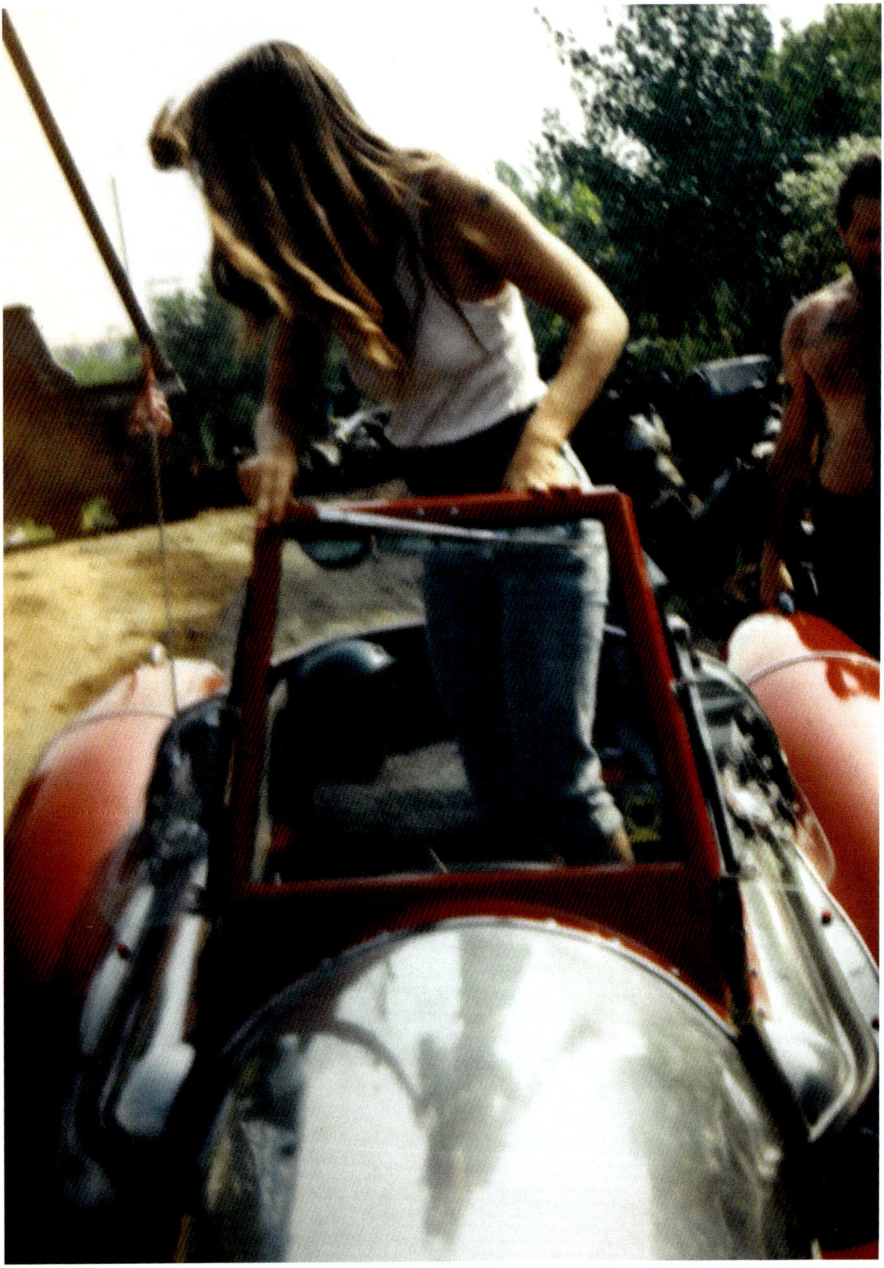

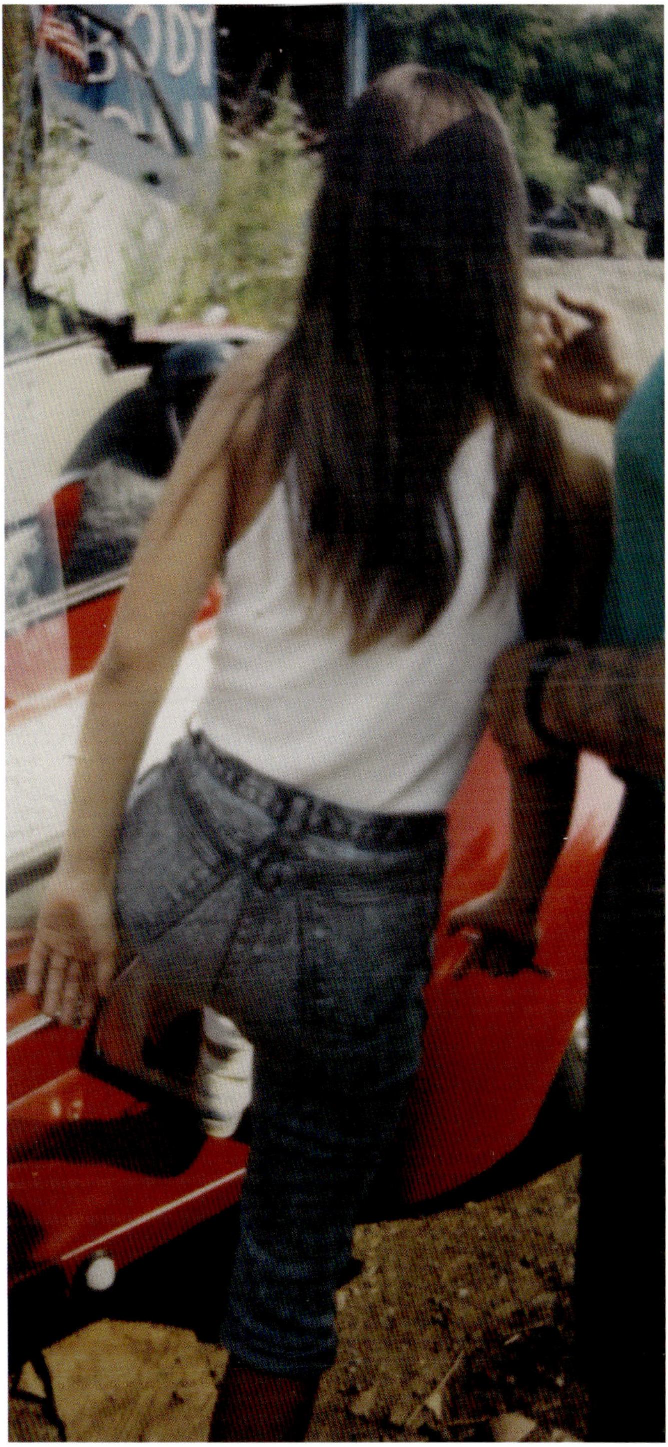

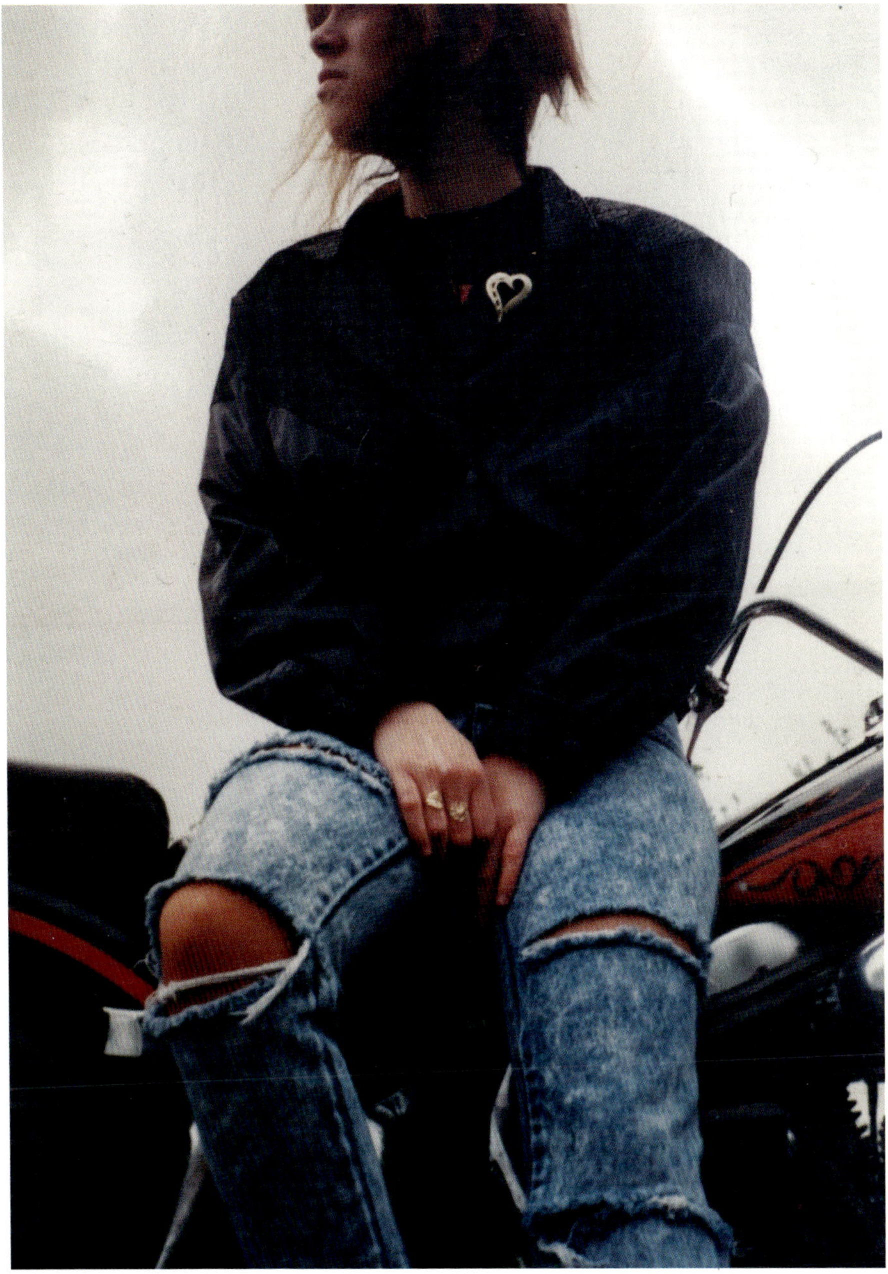

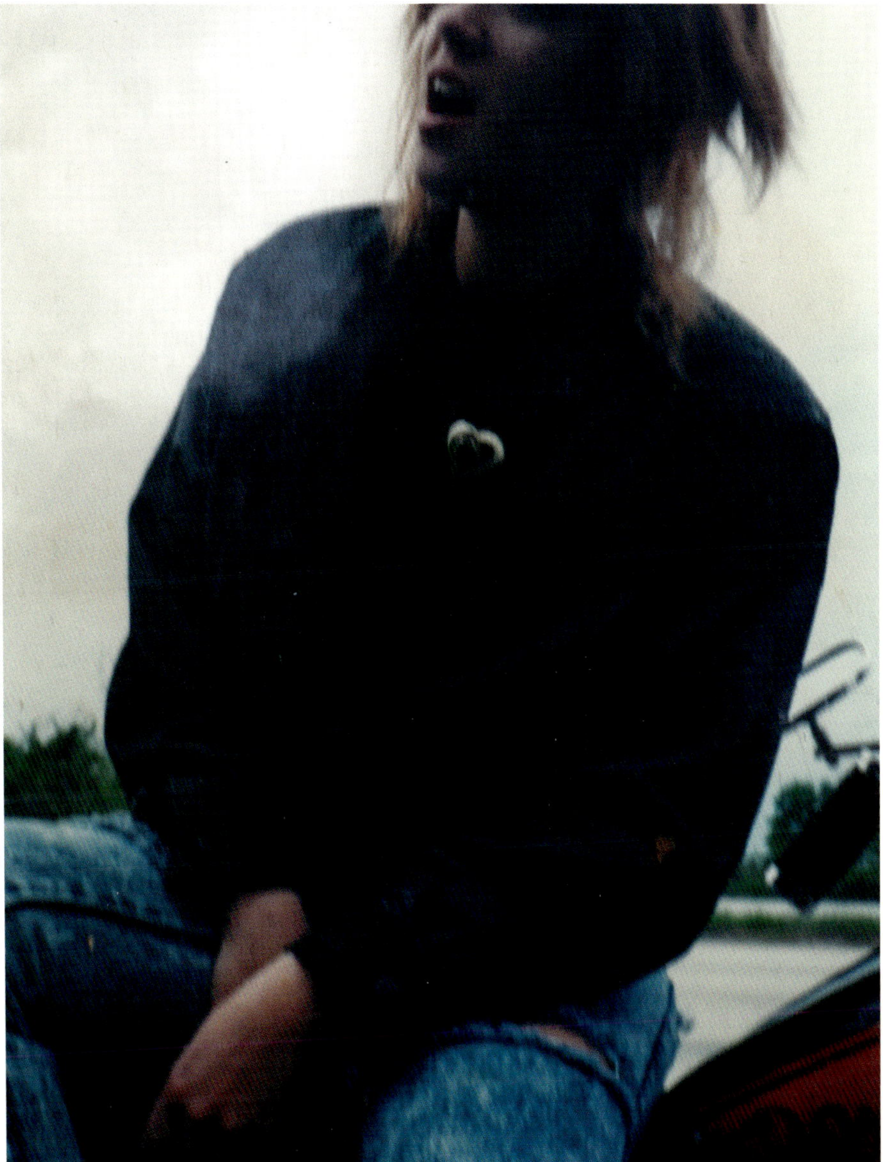

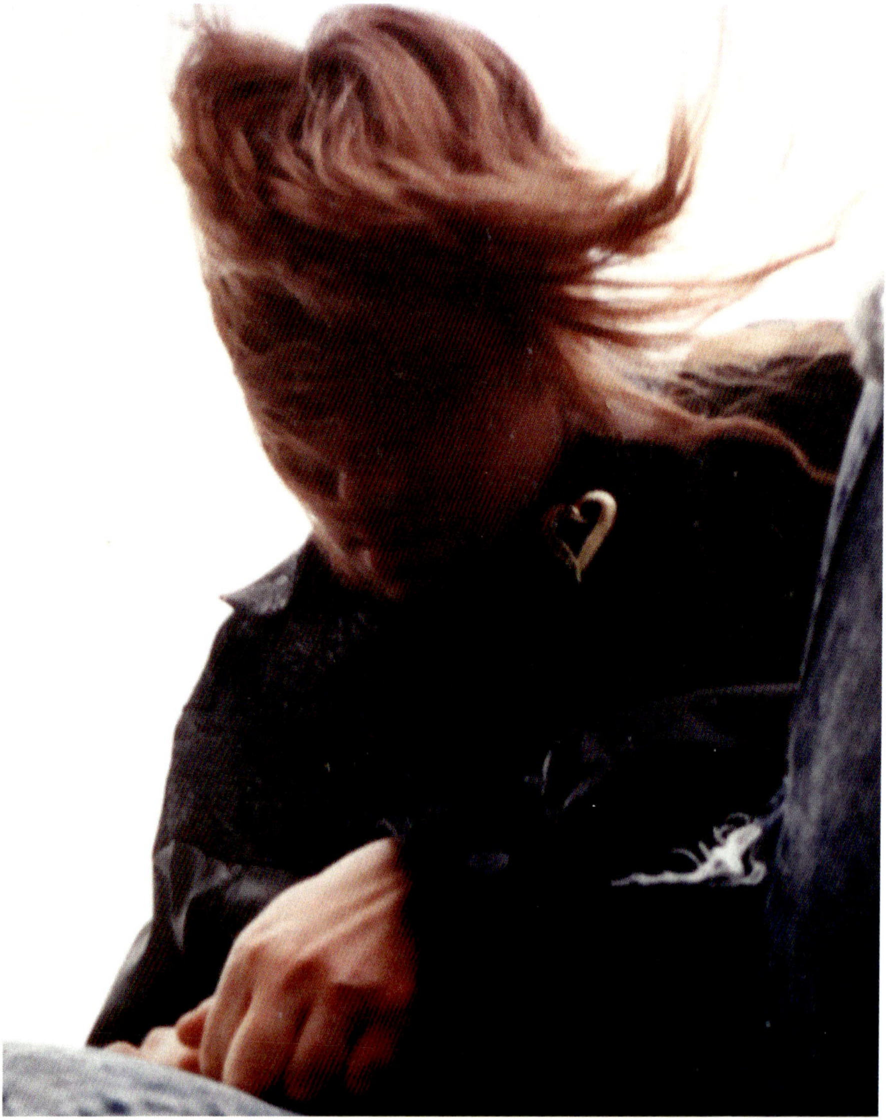

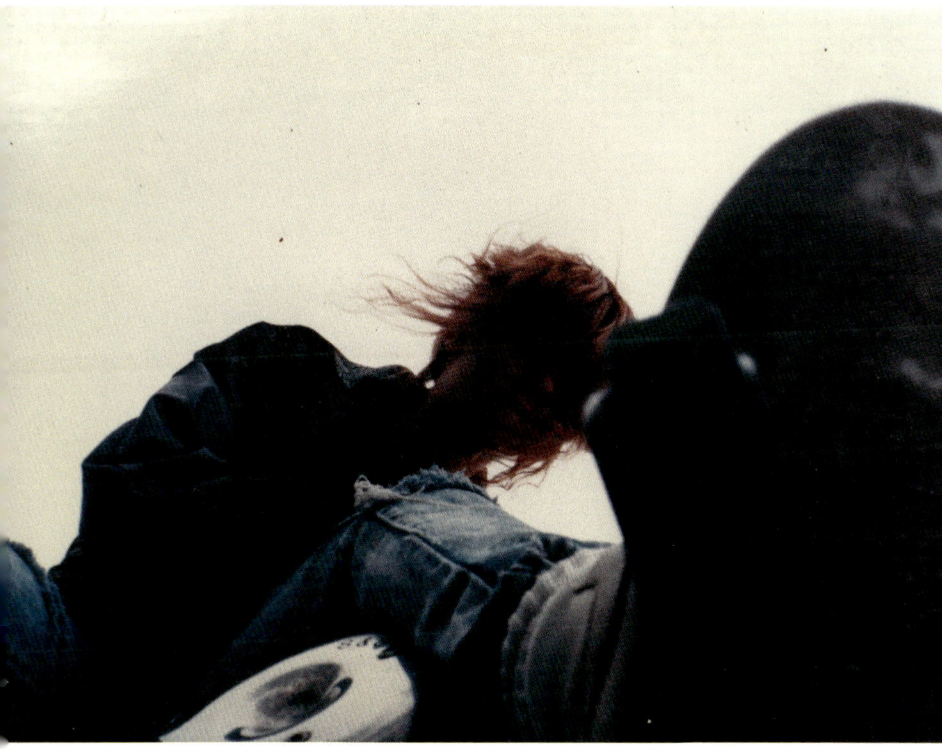

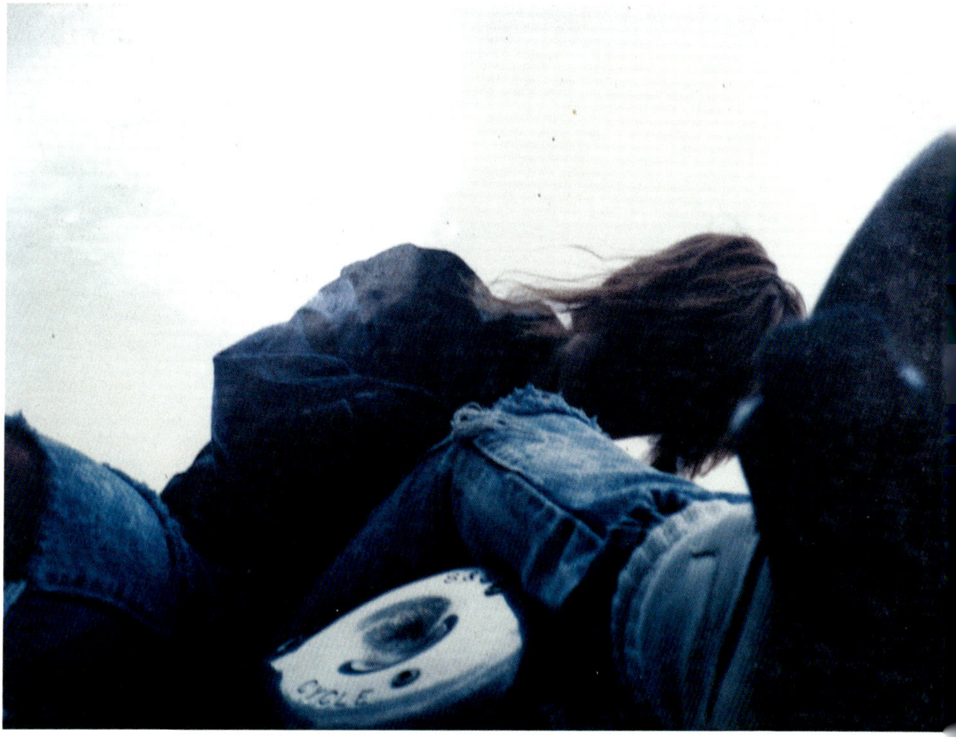

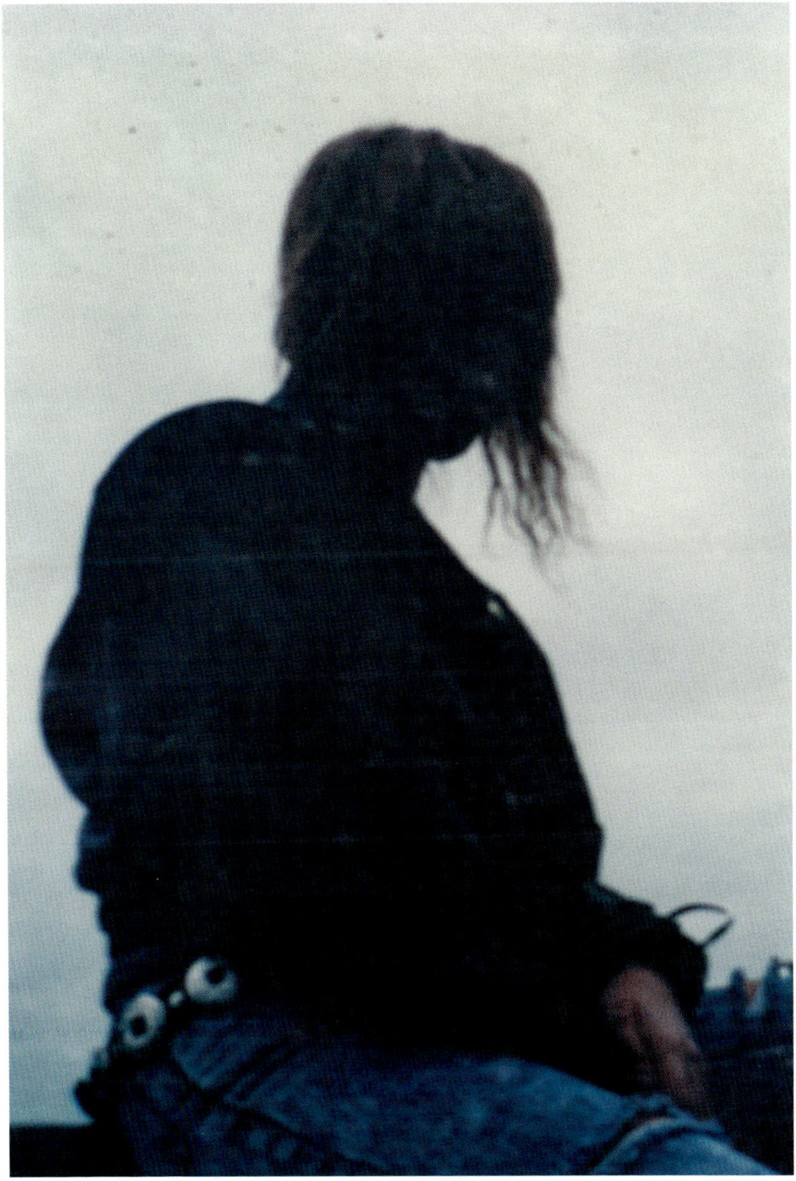

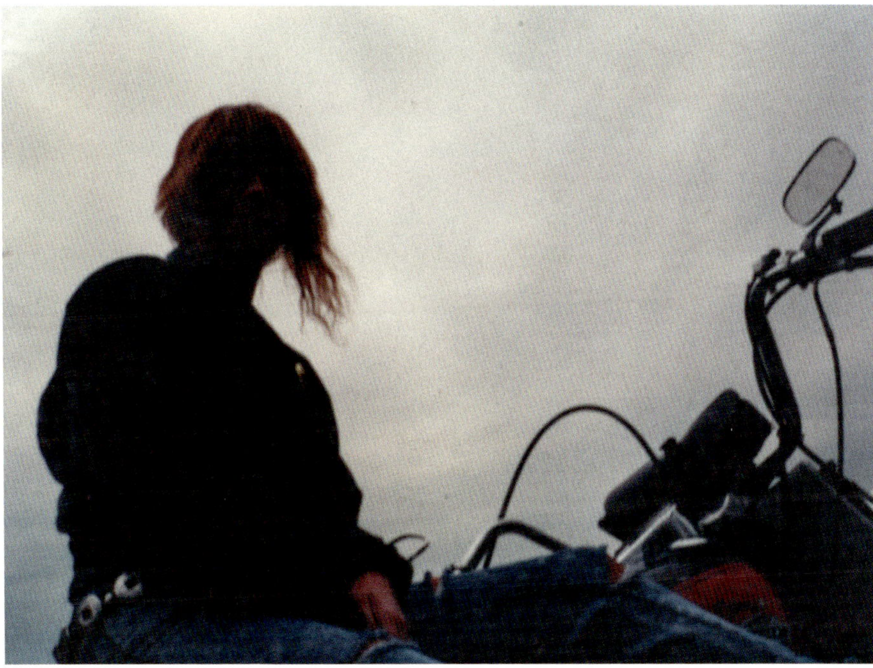

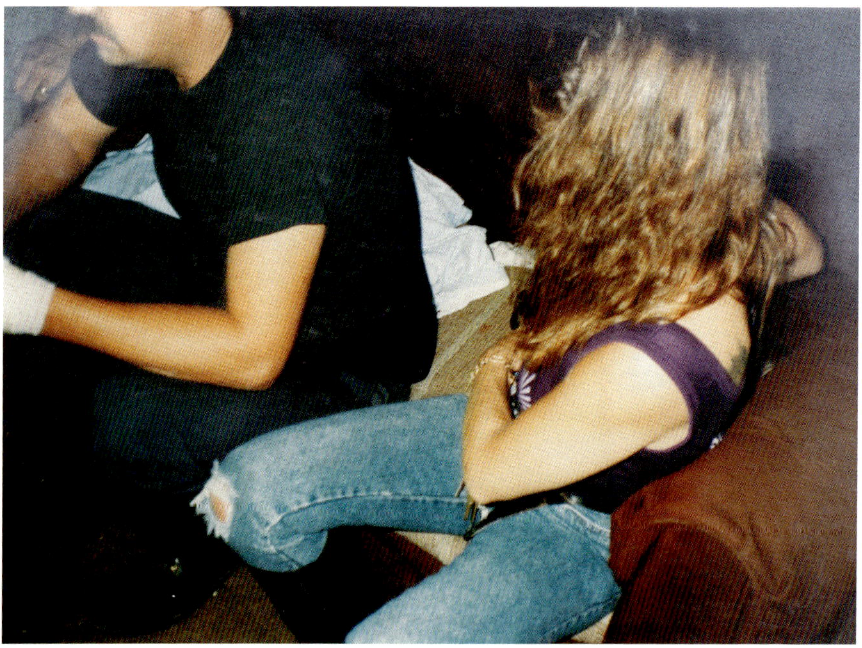

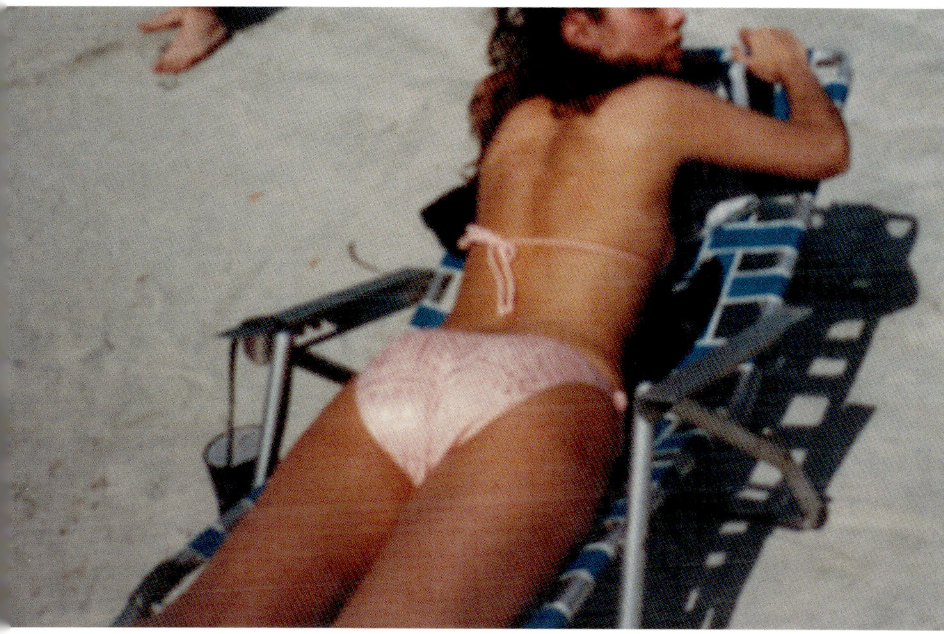

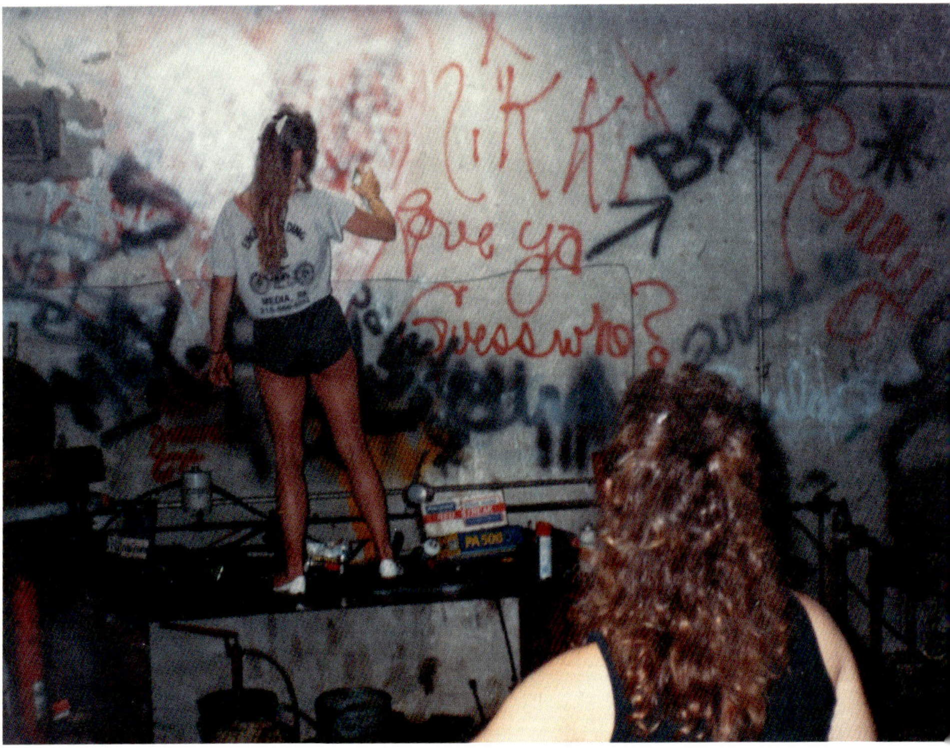
Love ya
Guess who?
PA 500

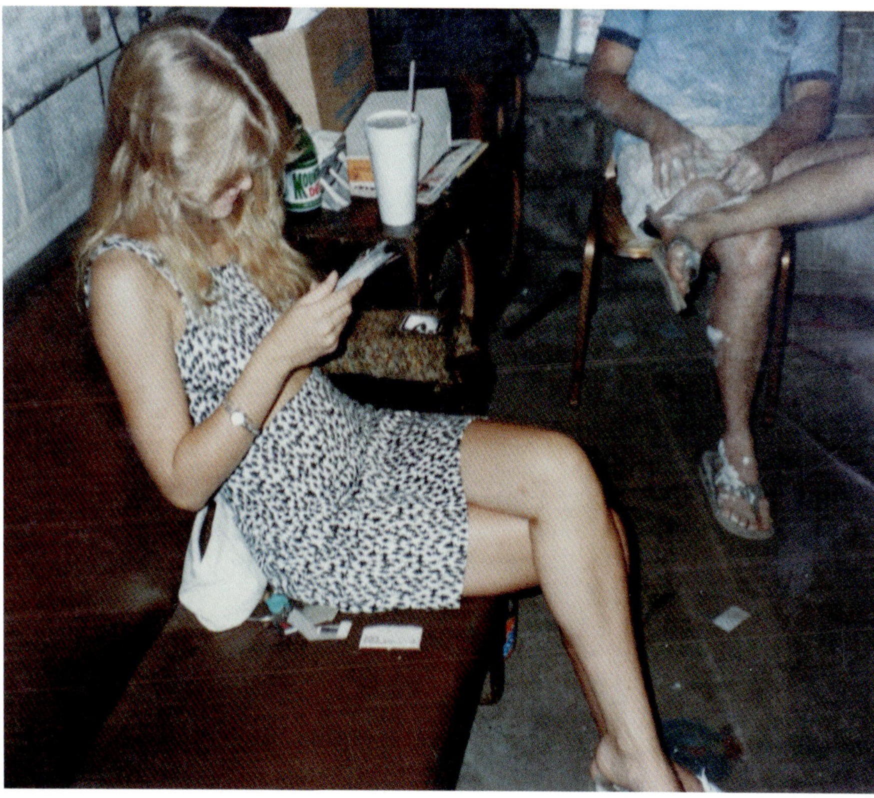

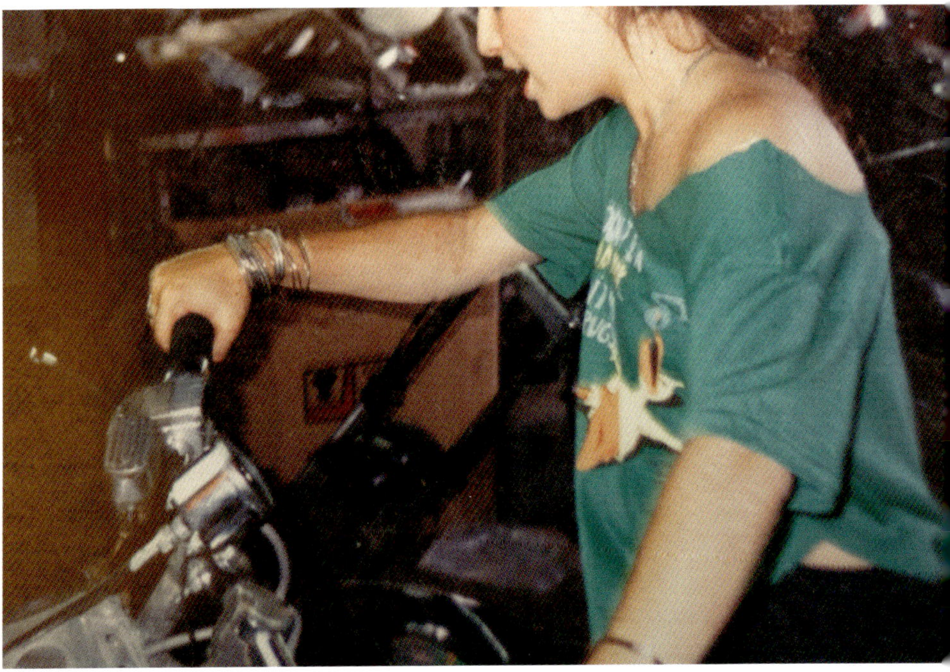

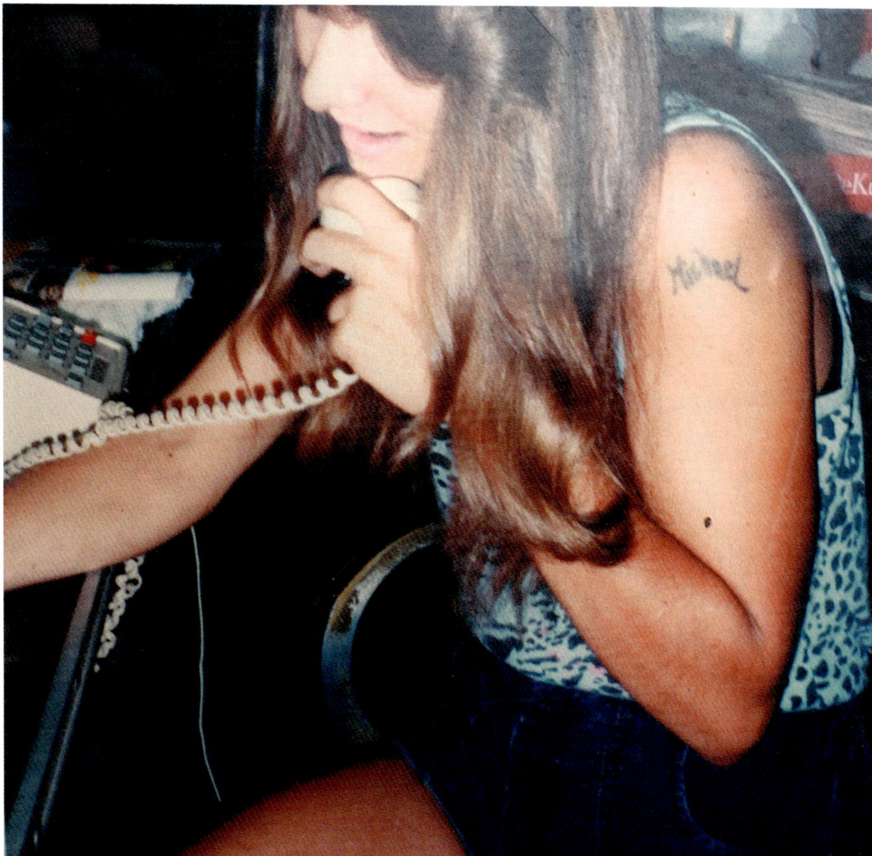

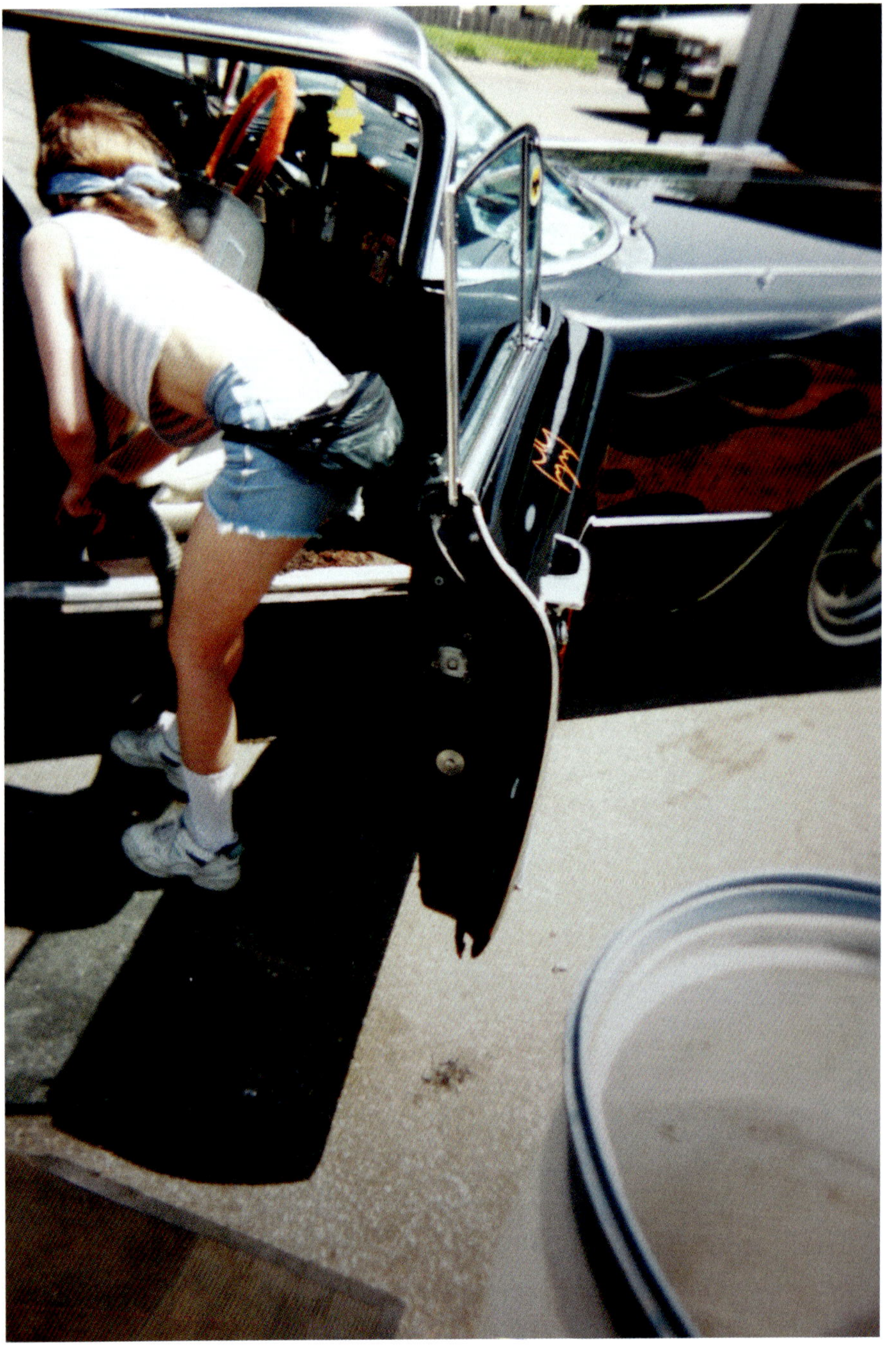

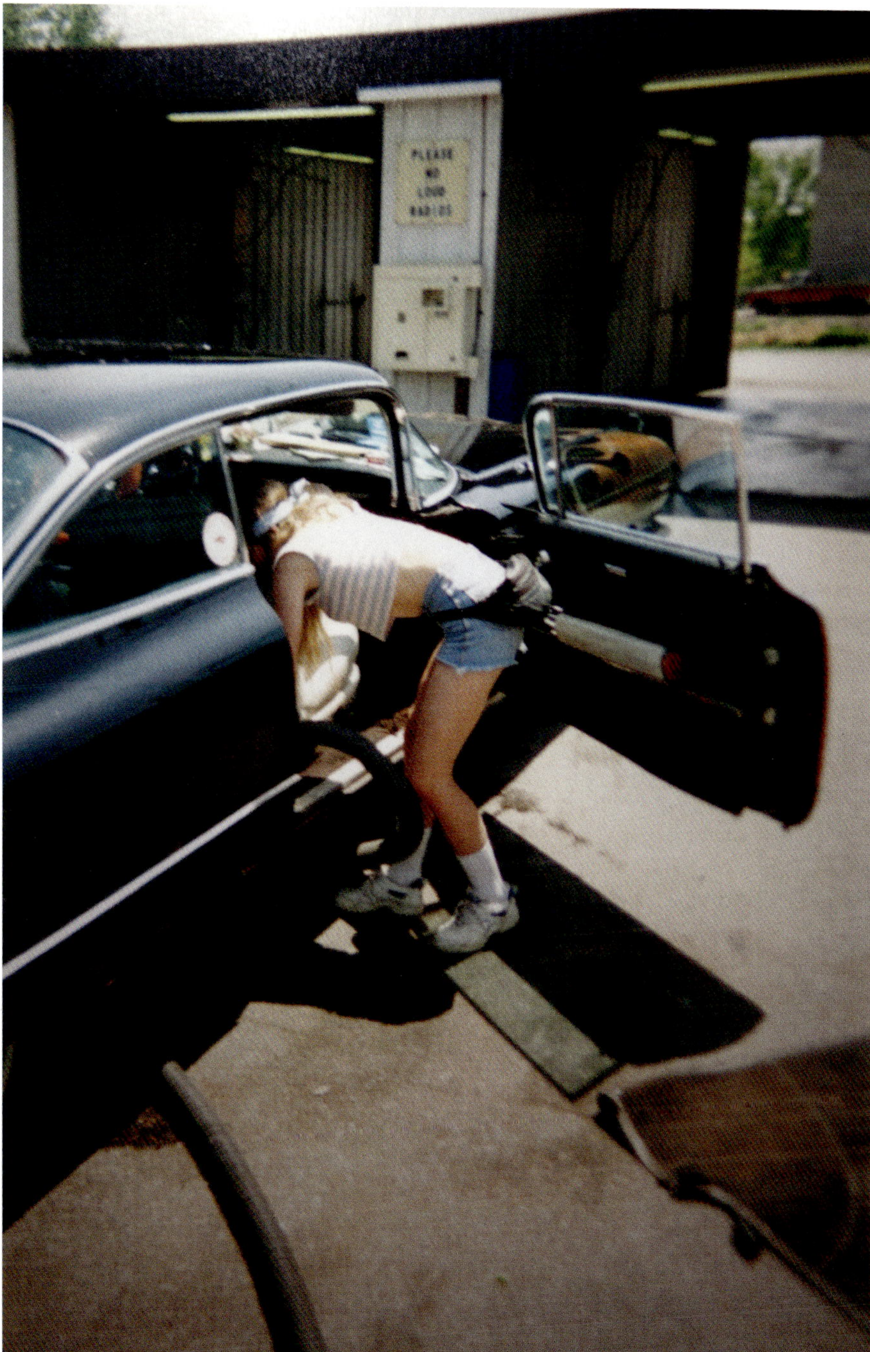
PLEASE
NO
LOUD
RADIOS

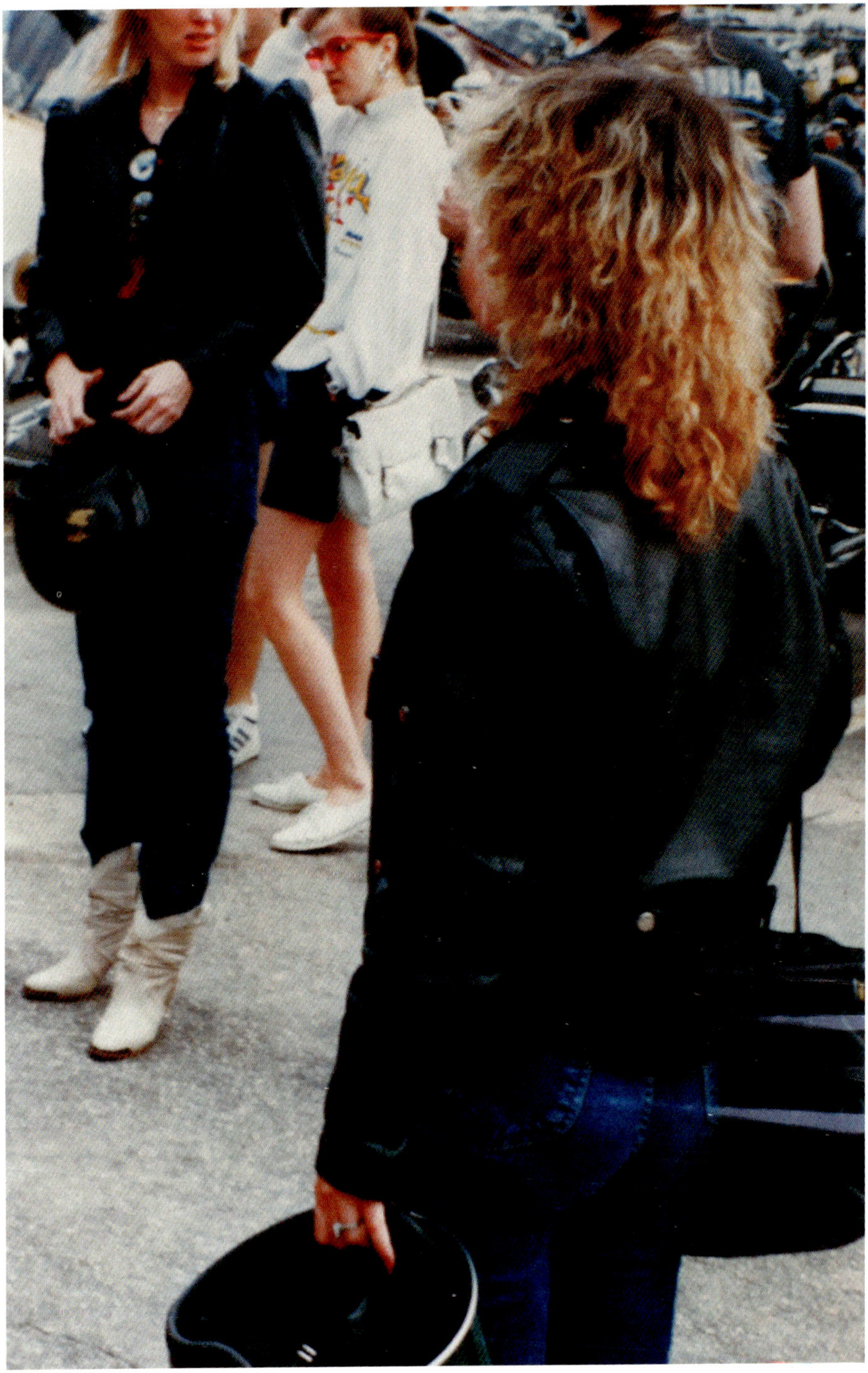

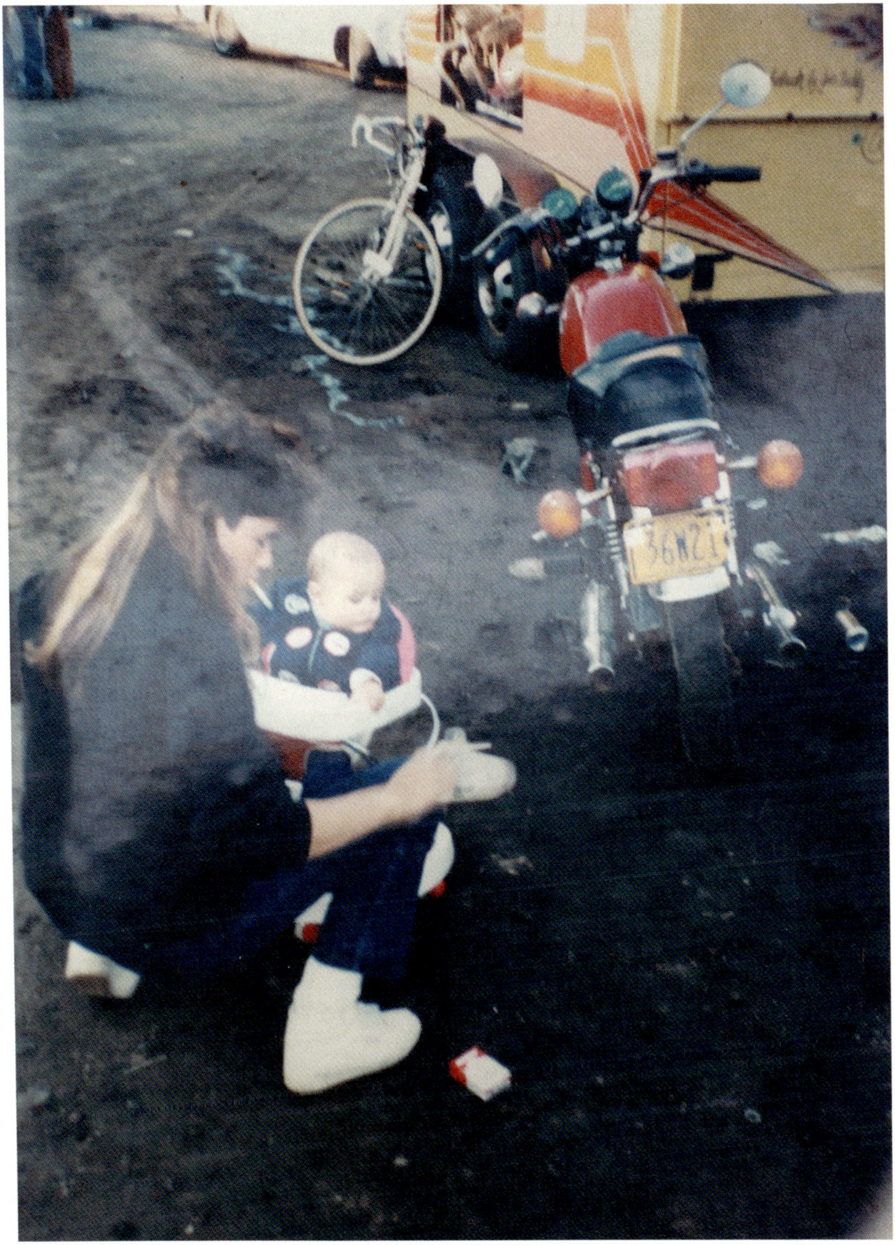

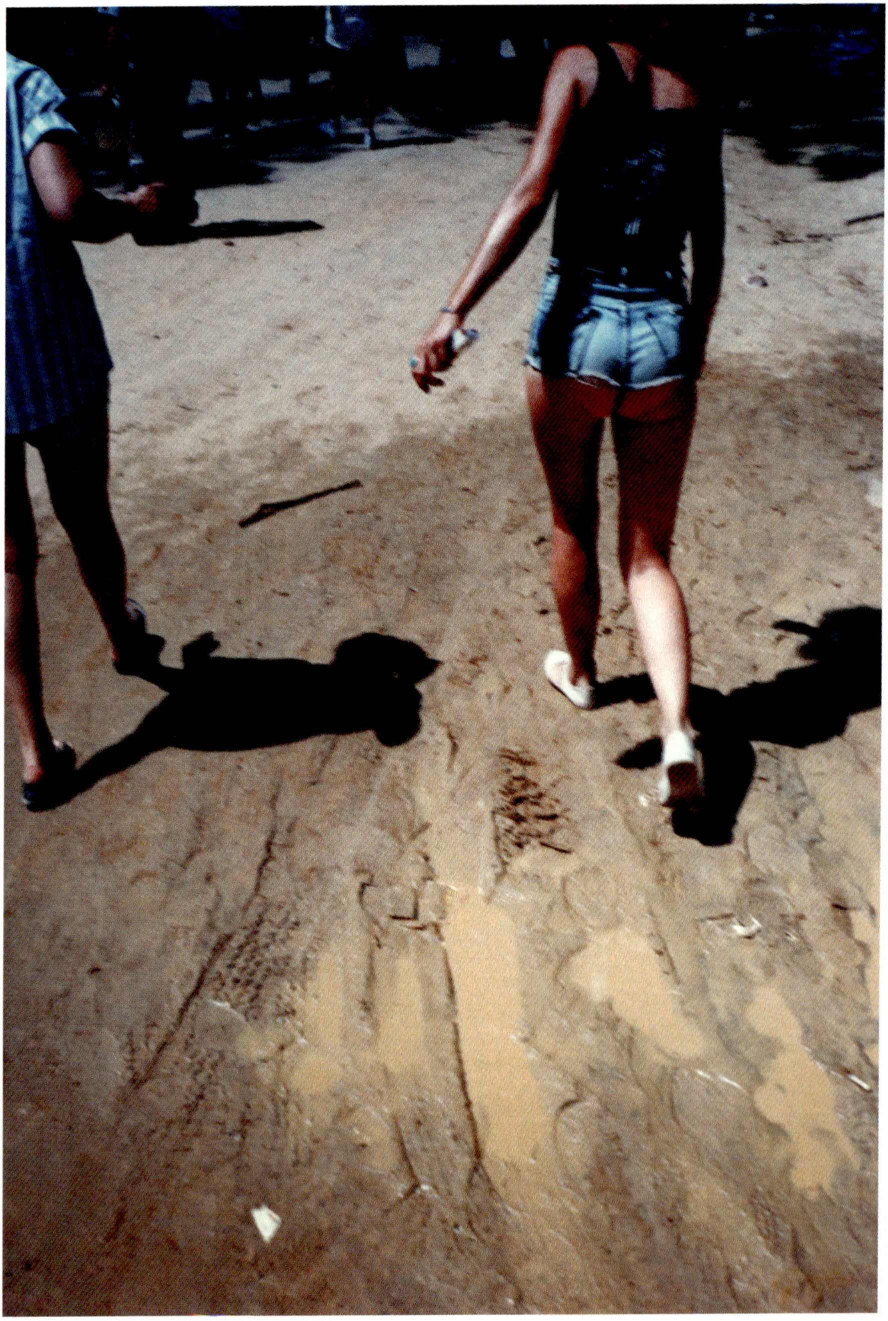

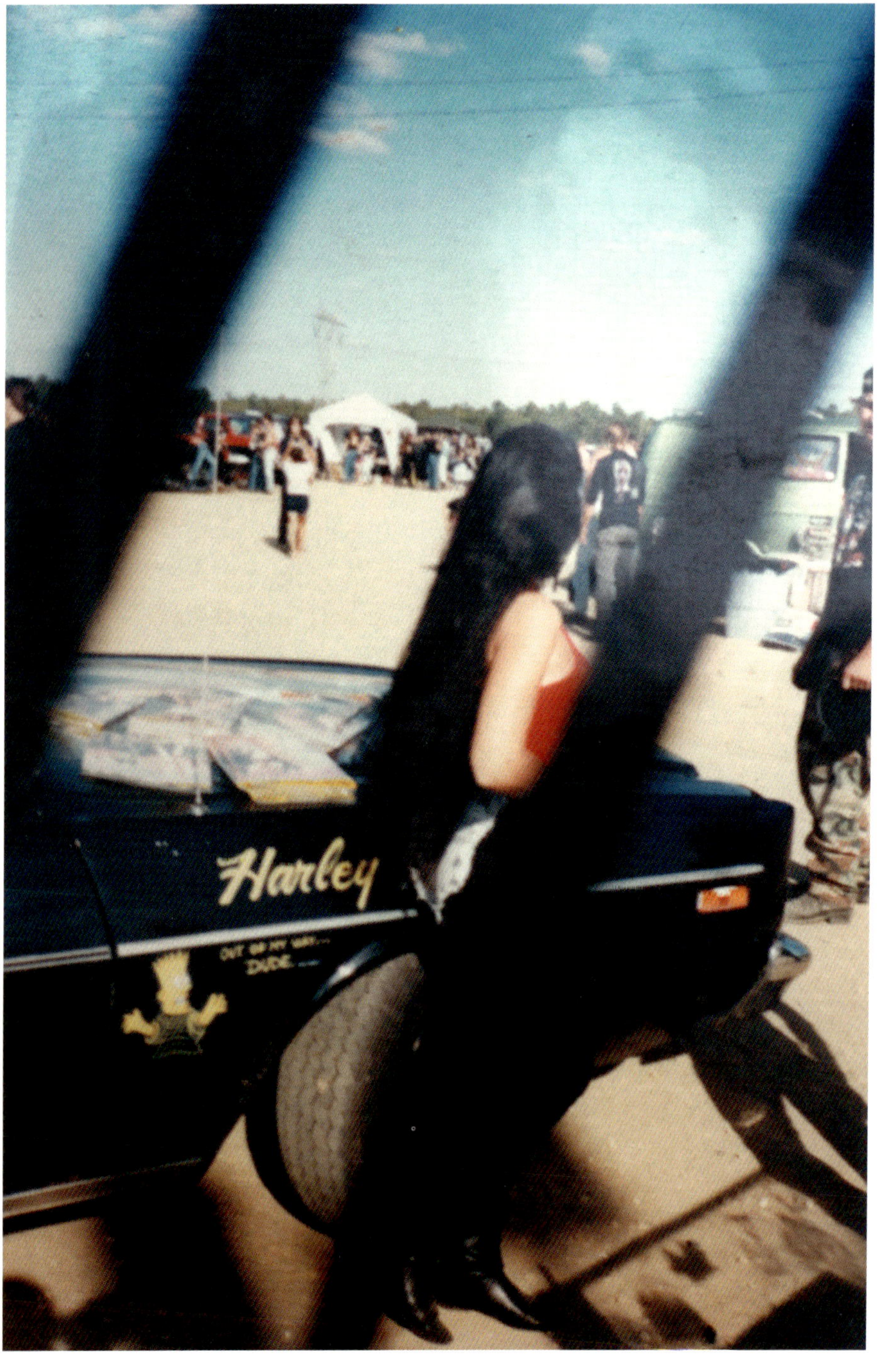
Harley

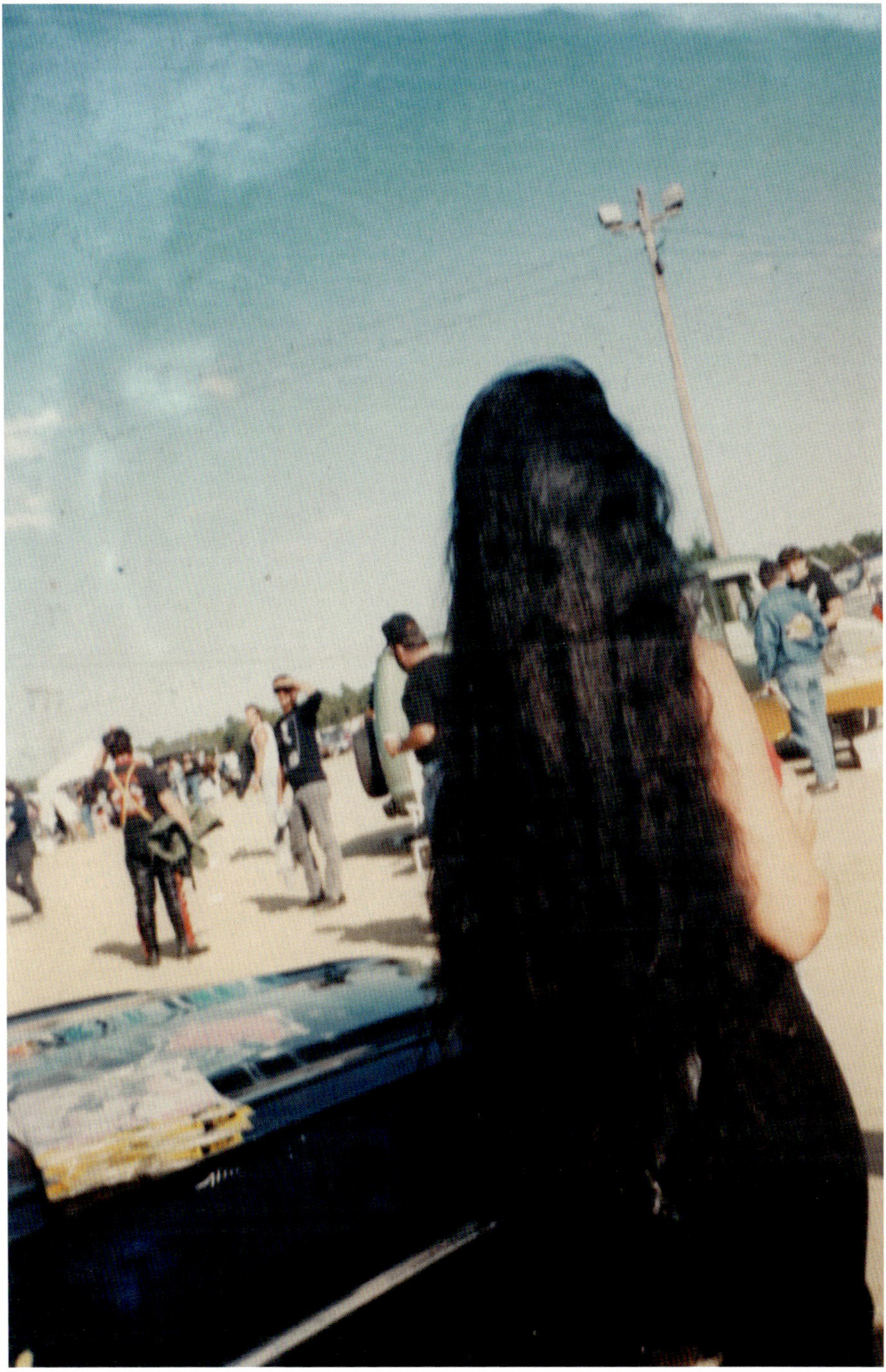

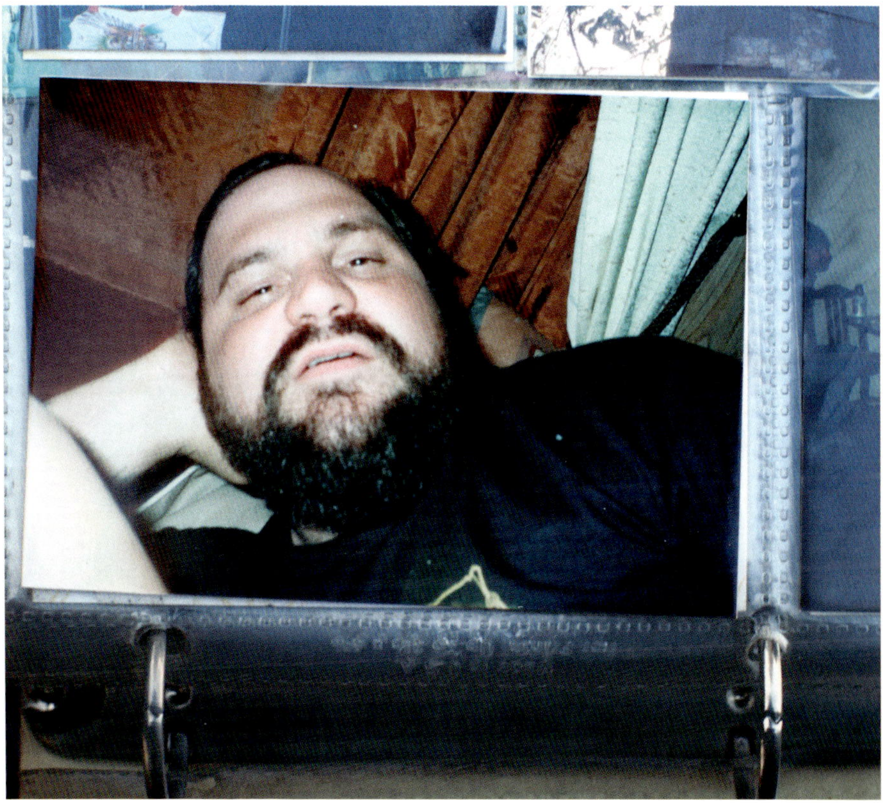

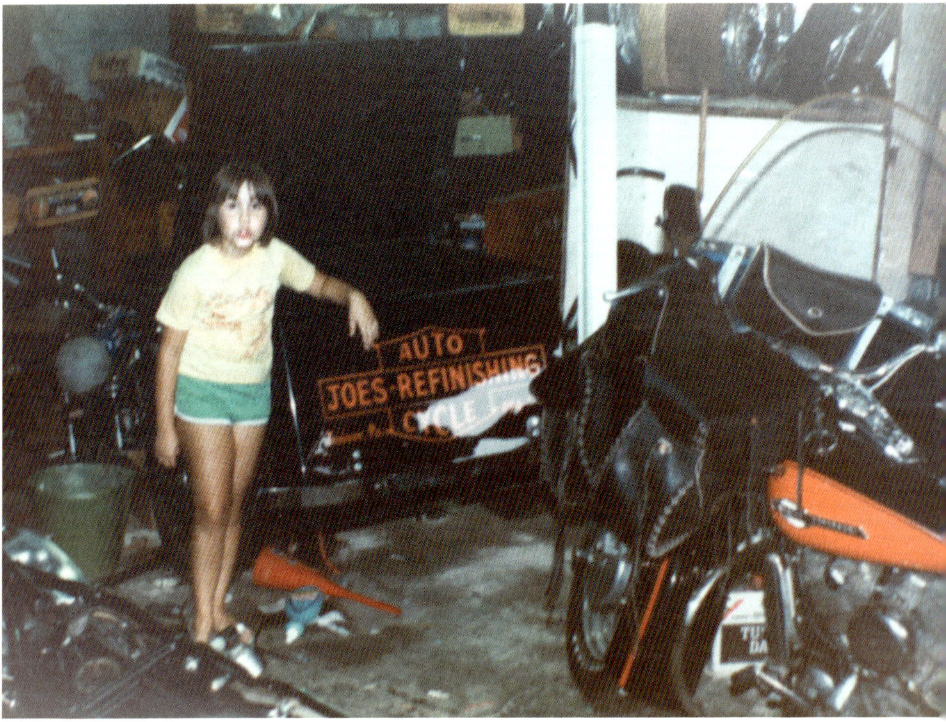
AUTO
JOES-REFINISHING

On the floor of my dad's closet in my grandmother's house sits a pile of crusty, taped-up, falling apart, magnetic-page albums. In them are his own pictures of his exploits as a biker in the Seventies and Eighties. I remember his camera, an SLR in a squarish, brown faux leather-covered cardboard case with a shoulder strap, one I would borrow as a teenager.

The photographs inside were of the beer parties, the motorcycle races, the dirtbike hillclimbs, and the women. I recognized some of these people and places and some of these events, but was baffled by a lot of what I saw. Who were these people? Where was I? Is this what my dad was doing when he disappeared after hours, my mom home with me and my sister? I knew my dad was partying, missing dinner, upsetting my mom, living a life of excess, spending the business cash that should have been used for bills, taxes and worker's comp. The drugs, the rock and roll.

Most of the women in these pictures are unrecognizable to me. I remember one from my childhood, and also the bimbo who my dad had in tow in his '56 Caddy when he showed up, hours late, to pick me and my friends up from the prom. But most of them were strangers to me. Yet I was impressed at how good some of the photos were. Inadvertently so? Or is this where I get a visual gene? There were the usual, expected, smiling shots, and the babes posing with a car or bike. But there were also the unexpected shots—the women stalked tenderly, seen from behind, the lens trained on the glints of light shimmering off their hair. The sort-of sweet portraits, the moment before or after they had exposed their breasts or tattoos to the camera. There were also the girls who appeared over and over again, and although they were unfamiliar to me, they clearly were a focus for him. And none of them were my mom, not in these photos anyway.

I was moved to re-photograph my father's images with my own camera, a digital SLR. The images herein are cropped, for both practical and conceptual reasons. In protecting the identities of the women pictured, I am also reiterating my relationship to them, which is none. To me—the 8 year old kid waiting for my dad to come home, wondering why he didn't want to be with us—the friends and fuckbuddies are anonymous, both real and not real, with no identities, no eyes, no thoughts. These women are as abstract as their existence in a child's mind.

—Lisa Kereszi